PAX AMERICANA !

PAX AMERICANA !

The war that lost Iraq its freedom

C R Irani

UBSPD
UBS Publishers' Distributors Pvt. Ltd.
New Delhi • Bhopal • Bangalore • Chennai
Ernakulam • Kolkata • Patna

UBS Publishers' Distributors Pvt. Ltd.
5 Ansari Road, **New Delhi-110 002**
Phones: 011-23273601, 23266646 • Fax: 23276593, 23274261
e-mail: ubspd@ubspd.com

143 M P Nagar, Zone I, **Bhopal-462 011**
Phones: 0755-5203183, 5203193, 2555228 • Fax: 2555285
e-mail: ubspdbhp@sancharnet.in

10 First Main Road, Gandhi Nagar, **Bangalore-560 009**
Phones: 080-2253903, 2263901, 2263902 • Fax: 2263904
e-mail: ubspdbng@eth.net

60 Nelson Manickam Road, Aminjikarai, **Chennai-600 029**
Phones: 044-23746222, 23746351-2 • Fax: 23746287
e-mail: ubspd@che.ubspd.com

No. 40/7940, Convent Road, **Ernakulam-682 035**
Phones: 0484-2353901, 2363905 • Fax: 2365511
e-mail: ubspd@che@eth.net

8/1-B Chowringhee Lane, **Kolkata-700 016**
Phones: 033-22521821, 22522910, 22529473 • Fax: 22523027
e-mail: ubspdcal@cal.vsnl.net.in

5 A Rajendra Nagar, **Patna-800 016**
Phones: 0612-2672856, 2673973, 2686170 • Fax: 2686169
e-mail: ubspdpat1@sancharnet.in

Distributors for Western India
M/s Preface Books
Unit No. 223 (2nd floor), Cama Industrial Estate,
Sun Mill Compound, Lower Parel (West), **Mumbai-400 013**
Phone: 022-4988054 ı Telefax: 022-24988048
e-mail: preface@prefacebooks.com

Visit us at www.ubspd.com & www.gobookshopping.com

©C.R. Irani

First Published   2003
First Reprint   2003
in arrangement with *The Statesman*, Kolkata

C.R. Irani asserts the moral right
to be identified as the author of this work.

All rights reserved. No part of this publication may be reproduced or transmitted in any form or by any means, electronic or mechanical, including photocopying, recording, or any information storage or retrieval system, without prior permission in writing from the publisher.

Editorial Consultant: Moitreyee Chatterjee

Cover Design: Dushyant Parasher

Typeset at: Instill Technologies, BE 277 Salt Lake, Kolkata 700 064

Printed at: Rajkamal Electric Press, New Delhi

For what avail the plough or sail
Or land or life, if freedom fail?

                                        Emerson

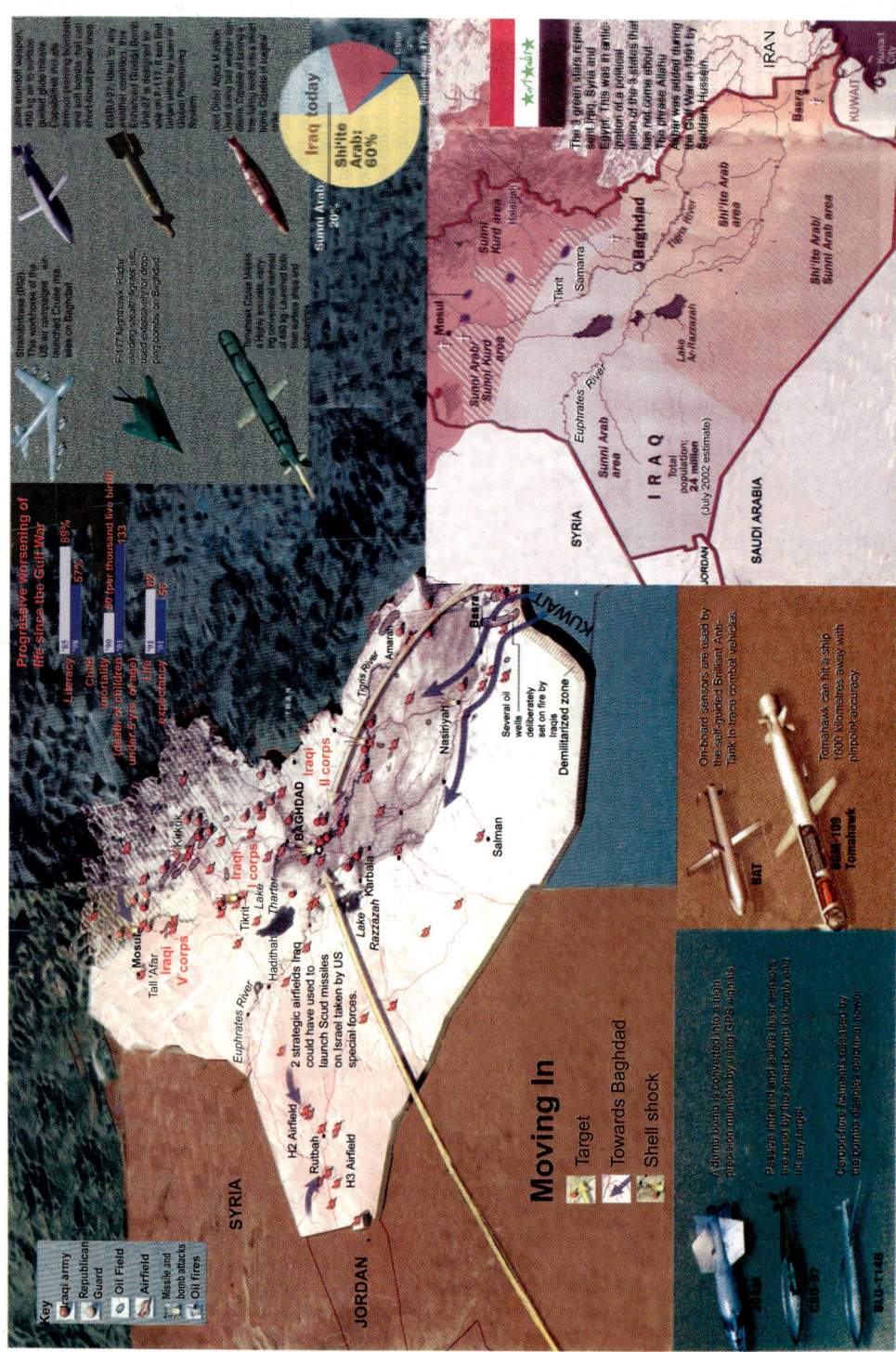

Contents

Introduction	ix
Dangerous Jingoism!	1
USA, Iraq & Iran	4
Problem of Bush!	7
Tilting at Windmills!	10
Our World Too!	13
Sharing the Spoils?	16
Retreat from Moscow!	19
Bringing up George!	22
International Brigand!	25
Omissions & Problems!	28
Dangerous Politician!	31
Powell Tries Hard!	34
Destination Disaster!	37
Tottering on the Brink	41
Bush's Frustration	44
On a Razor's Edge!	47
Tony's Goose Cooked!	51
Bush's Grubby War!	54
Bush's Law!	58
Anglo-American Dilemma	62

Iraq Fights for Survival!	65
Chickens Home to Roost	69
Saddam's Lucky Number	72
Hand it to Bush!	75
Exploding Myths and More	79
New Fundamentalism	85
Thumping the Table!	88
And now Journalists!	92
Calling the Price!	95
Our Way of Life	99
Catastrophic Success!	104
Iraq is not a Game!	107
In the Sands of Time!	111
Cold Feet over Iraq!	115
The Rest of the World!	119
Epilogue	123
Iraq—Over the Years	131

Introduction

Despite vociferous protests to the contrary from President George Bush and Prime Minister Tony Blair, there can be no doubt that the American-led invasion of Iraq, with Britain in tow, was illegal, in breach of International Law and in brazen defiance of the United Nations and the expressed wish of the Security Council, not to speak of a majority of the five veto-wielding powers. An exact parallel for the Anglo-American outrage, however, does exist and must, in fairness, be noted. Saddam Hussein was in similar breach of International Law when he invaded Kuwait, on 3 August 1990. But here the similarity ends. Saddam was more straightforward. He said Kuwait i oil was his because he said so and sent in the Iraqi army to enforce his claim. He was driven out by the united will of the international community acting under the authority of the United Nations and its Charter and of the Security Council, which passed an unanimous resolution, Number 678 of 29 November 1990, to drive Iraq out of Kuwait. However, Saddam did not say that Kuwait was hiding weapons of mass destruction to threaten the world; that he, Saddam, was going to liberate Kuwaitis from the Amir and enforce democracy; nor did he say that he was intervening to make sure that Kuwaiti oil was used only for the benefit of the Kuwaiti people. Hypocrisy of this order was reserved for those who until recently were claiming the moral high ground in international affairs—United States of America and Great Britain.

This compilation of Editorials and Caveats carried by *The Statesman* newspaper documents and tells the story of the twists and turns in extremely traumatic events and exposes the premeditated intention of the United States to go to war. President Bush said as early as his State of the Union message in January 2002 that 'Iran, Iraq, and North Korea formed an axis of evil'. His focus however, remained on Iraq. In quick succession, he fabricated other reasons in his troubled mind to go after Saddam. 'That man tried to kill my Dad in 1993', he said. When weapons inspectors were asked to return to Iraq, Saddam accepted them but Bush insisted it would serve no purpose. At one point, a day before Hans Blix, Chief Weapons Inspector, was to give yet another report to the Security Council, Bush's National Security Advisor, Condoleezza Rice, part of his inner circle, visited him and tried to influence him to hold Saddam in material breach of his obligations. Confident that her mission was successful, the White House put out a story of what Blix would say in his report. Blix ignored the crude pressure tactics and reported faithfully that there was improvement in Iraq's attitude and that the work of the inspectors should continue. On 12 September 2002, Bush addressed the United Nations, using the occasion to abuse Saddam and declaring that only force would disarm Iraq. A month later, the State Department spokesman had to concede that America

Introduction

would, after all, come back to the Security Council if weapons inspectors reported that Saddam was not cooperating. All reports of the inspectors said that Iraq was indeed cooperating but they were brushed aside because they were inconvenient. Bush followed up with an ultimatum to Saddam to leave Baghdad and go into exile within forty-eight hours or face war. This decision was an intensely private one, not mentioned to the Security Council and no approval was sought.

Tony Blair was not to be left behind. Under his personal authority he put out a dossier on Iraq's alleged weapons of mass destruction and charged Iraq with non-compliance. It turned out that it was gleaned from the Internet and said to have been based on 'top secret' intelligence, prompting the instant retort that if it was top secret what was it doing on the Internet anyway! The stubbornly held American position was to have a single resolution in the Security Council authorising the use of force, the moment the head of the weapons inspection team reported that Saddam was not cooperating. No nation apart from the United States had any stomach for such an outrage. Bush had to give way and the result was Resolution 1441. He had to agree that in the event of an adverse report from the weapons inspectors, the matter would come back to the Security Council and it would be for the Council to proceed further as may be dictated by circumstances at that time. Soon thereafter in October 2002, the State Department's official spokesman reiterated at a regular press conference that America would return to the Security Council if weapons inspectors were not satisfied that Saddam was cooperating. This solemn commitment was flouted with contempt. The written response of Iraq as required by the inspectors—all 12,000 pages of it—was physically waylaid by the United States before it could reach the Security Council, saying they wished to study it first. When America and Britain launched their attack on Iraq, Hans Blix resigned his position accusing the United States of a premeditated desire to go to war. Blix's courage does him credit. He could not have forgotten that his team was used to get Saddam to destroy 70 of his 100 odd Al-Samoud missiles ahead of the invasion. If Saddam had been able to keep them he would have given a better account of himself. The heroism of the Iraqi people is now for the history books.

Well after the invasion began, the distinguished Ambassador of the United States of America to India, Robert D Blackwill, published a signed piece in another newspaper in Delhi on 8 April 2003 advancing an unstateable proposition—that Resolutions 678, 687 and 1441 authorised war without further ado, anyway. Resolution 678 authorised evicting Iraq from Kuwait; it is absurd to quote it as authority to wage another war more than a decade later and in different circumstances. Resolution 687 dealt with the post Gulf war situation in 1992 and had no application. Finally if Resolution 1441 already authorised war, would America and Britain explain why they tried so valiantly to get another and specific resolution? Ambassador Blackwill says it was "to take the extra step", provoking a response in the Caveat— *Calling the Price! of 13 April 2003* that afterthoughts were no substitute for argument!

America seems to have become unhinged after 11 September. Men of straw distinguished by fanaticism matched only by Osama bin Laden and Islamic extremists, are abroad—President Bush and his avaricious gang, Cheney, Rumsfeld, Perle, even Powell, raised cheers for their disregard of international opinion, of International

Law and even of plain decency and honesty, from captive audiences. President Bush claimed the support of some 30 countries for his war on Iraq. He was immediately challenged. His Ambassador in Delhi quickly raised it to 'about 50'. There are two answers to this. One, that right and wrong, good and evil, lawful and illegal, are matters of principle judged by objective and universally accepted criteria; they cannot be settled by how many countries are persuaded to vote 'aye' or 'nay'. It reminds me of the habit of politicians in India who, if worsted in courts of law, declare with complete assurance that they will turn their backs on the law that so disappoints them and appeal instead to the 'people's court' whose verdict they can manipulate by a victory in elections. Here we are up against that most distressing of human frailties, the closed mind, which men of the religious right in America like President Bush hold in common with the likes of Osama bin Laden. I record with satisfaction that the International Press Institute has publicly criticised the United States for having included in their 'Coalition of the Willing', obnoxious repressive regimes like, Azerbaijan, Georgia, Ethiopia, Eritrea, and Uzbekistan. IPI goes on to tell the UK and the USA that they are not only damaging their own human rights reputations, but also condoning the actions of these countries. Has America sunk so low? Do values count for nothing when weighed against barrels of stolen oil?

Gulf War I, fought by George Bush senior was reported by correspondents of high caliber and integrity. Peter Arnett was the doyen of the corps. This time he was summarily sacked by NBC on instructions from the Pentagon and under pressure from George Bush. Peter's crime was to question the war aims of America and the tactics employed. London's *Daily Mail* newspaper promptly offered him another job and it is comforting to know that Britain has not descended into the dungeons as swiftly as America seems to have done. And that Tony Blair is powerless to accelerate such a process. May he never acquire such power! For over a decade, I have opposed within UNESCO the concerted efforts of autarkic regimes to legitimize government interference in the media, encapsulated in the New World Information Order, a Cold War concept. I freely record, the cooperation I received in this task from American and British colleagues, as Chairman of IPI. Now it seems that I must come to their aid. British cabinet ministers are systematically undermining the reporting of the BBC on the war in Iraq, roundly accusing it of distorting the public's perception of the war. It is the British government's sense of values that is distorted and that by visions of unlimited supplies of cheap oil from Iraq. Let it be said openly—*The BBC has both a right and an absolute duty to report on this war. It is vital to the viewing public that they receive a plurality of views in order to understand what is happening in Iraq. The UK government must accept that the best people to decide news are not politicians but the broadcasters themselves.* It is a thousand pities that countries like the USA and the UK, which in the last century set an example to others in the struggle for free speech should now so forget themselves as to give priority to a mess of pottage over principles. Americans tend to hold that if you do not have the equivalent of the First Amendment to their Constitution, which has been such an inspiration to the rest of the world, you have no hope of enjoying rights of free speech and expression. I have always protested at this oversimplification. In the light of current experience, I have to suggest that in the First Amendment, after the words— "Congress shall pass no law ..." the following words be

Introduction

inserted "... and the President shall take no action ... ". Of a piece with this new and bogus nationalism, was the attack on foreign journalists quartered in the Palestine Hotel in Baghdad by American tanks. And why—because someone saw a camera pointed at a tank from a window of the Palestine Hotel! Is a camera a weapon of mass destruction? The outrage was compounded by deliberate attacks on different premises of Al-Jazeera and Abu Dhabi TV stations, which were doing their professional duty of holding up a mirror to the suffering caused by American cluster bombs and other weapons of mass destruction and beaming the pictures into American homes. It must be a sobering thought for America and Britain that CNN for sure and even to an extent the BBC, now rank below AFP of France, as a reliable purveyor of information.

Bush has claimed the right of a preemptive strike on Iraq on no better ground than suspicion. Has this terrible man any sense of the precedent he is setting? He seems already in the middle of a compendium of his own on terrorism! Iraq was harbouring terrorists because some 'suspicious looking' men travelled through Baghdad and were 'bound to have made contact' with Saddam Hussein. Syria has chemical weapons; Colin Powell has had to rush post haste to Damascus to repair the damage caused by his President's words. Syria is also accused of sheltering Saddam, family and friends because Bush cannot find Saddam any more than he can find Osama bin Laden. His stupidity, married to his greed, is making America the laughing stock of the world. It should ring all kinds of alarm bells in Washington that Iraq's neighbours have met and asked Washington to take itself and its troops out of Iraq forthwith. Furthermore, that the meeting was held on Saudi soil. The Wahabi dynasty in Saudi Arabia cannot exist for a day without American protection; yet they have felt obliged to ask America to get lost. The wider Arab world has placed Bush neatly on the horns of a cruel dilemma. They have tabled a resolution in the Security Council to eliminate all nuclear weapons from the entire Middle East region. Their target is Israel, which has nuclear weapons. Are nuclear bombs weapons of individual destruction? Bush cannot be seen to oppose the elimination of nuclear weapons and he cannot tell Israel to disarm any more than he can fly. Further afield Bush thinks North Korea's programme of openly producing nuclear weapons is a 'regional problem' to be tackled differently and at leisure, while Pakistan's proven sponsorship of terrorism in Kashmir is a matter for 'dialogue' between India and 'steadfast ally', Pakistan.

The US Commander in Iraq is on record as saying that finding Iraq's weapons of mass destruction may take months or years. Russia has called checkmate by insisting that sanctions imposed on Iraq which limits the amount of oil that can be extracted, can only be lifted after weapons inspectors certify that Iraq is free of prohibited weapons. This is a neat manoeuvre and Bush does not know which way to turn. If inspectors return and confirm that Iraq does not have weapons of mass destruction, the major excuse for the war disappears and Bush and Blair qualify as war criminals. It is also a tremendous loss of face. An increasingly desperate Bush may well add to the many illegalities he has committed and grab the oil wells anyway. This is bound to set the cat among the pigeons. His immediate response is that if the weapons are not there, he, Bush, is prepared to certify that Saddam would have developed them in six months! Therefore he was right to go to war. Television is a pitiless medium. To see and hear Bush suddenly expound this asinine view is an education in itself; it shows Bush as being extraordinarily

Introduction

proud of his discovery—perhaps in his mind equal in importance to the discovery of Einstein's theory of relativity!

In the ultimate analysis the United States is a functioning democracy. Its carefully balanced Federal Constitution has never before had to put up with a President whose selection rather than election was so thoroughly questionable. For the first time in living memory it is possible to question whether the famed system of checks and balances in the governance of the United States will work. I say it will because there are hopeful signs emerging although it is possible to be impatient with the process. It will accelerate if the American economy, which was struggling anyway and is now in serious trouble, cannot obtain large infusions of Iraqi oil very quickly. The Security Council is in no mood to lift sanctions and allow unlimited quantities of oil to flow to ease Bush's pain. France and Russia, which are owed millions by Iraq, are being subjected to intense pressure to cooperate or bid good-bye to the money owing to them. Chirac and Putin can run rings round Bush and his grubby oilmen. Both must calculate how long it will take for America to regain its equilibrium. On that judgment will depend their response.

Included in this compendium are two perceptive pieces by Jeremy Seabrook who writes regularly for *The Statesman* from London. They provide a worthwhile underpinning to this war, its causes and effects. I would have liked to include the excellent piece by Simon Jenkins, former editor of *The Times,* London, who has some advice for the United Nations so cruelly used by America and Britain. Unfortunately copyright difficulties in carrying it in this compilation have stood in the way. Readers will see a reference to it in the Caveat—*Calling the*

Price! published on 13 April 2003 and if you wish to read the full piece, which I recommend, you will find it in *The Statesman* of 10 April 2003.

The entire concept of this book, everything associated with its editorial content, and getting it ready for the press has been undertaken by Moitreyee Chatterjee, the talented and painstaking editor, who has looked upon this project as a labour of love. Overcoming my initial diffidence, I have agreed to let the book go forward and have even written the Introduction and the Epilogue, at her persuasion—the first time in my life that I have written anything on instructions! If this offering meets with your approval the entire credit must go to Moitreyee. My young colleague Ishan Joshi, Editorial Coordinator of *The Statesman,* has met her several requests with his characteristic aplomb and a sense of fun. It has improved the book and I acknowledge his contribution.

I have one further thought. It has given me no pleasure to write these pieces; I wish they did not have to be written. But my duty to my profession and to readers of the newspaper I have the honour to edit, leave me no choice. If there is one lesson that these teach us, it is the sobering thought of how easy it is to subordinate principles and values one has lived by to crass commercial considerations. This is the thought uppermost in my mind as I try to understand why people I have known and respected in America and Britain have fallen so low. *And what a fall there was, my countrymen!*

Kolkata   C R Irani
16 May 2003

Dangerous Jingoism!

Bush's State of the Union

The utterly unacceptable rhetoric of the American President, first in his highly visible State of the Union address to Congress, repeated a day later in Atlanta, must have provided Bush some satisfaction, if he goes by the hysterical applause he received. He said that 'Iran, Iraq and North Korea formed an axis of evil' in the context of terrorism. The merits of his outburst are easily disposed of. That North Korea once had a programme of developing nuclear weapons is not denied; but that was a long time ago. Colin Powell should have told him that dusting off the files of the Reagan era and mistaking them for red-hot reports of current events brings the office of the President into disrepute as being hopelessly out of date. In fact the South Korean President, Kim dae Jung has established relations with the North following the new leadership in Pyongyang and is making slow but steady progress. He will now feel let down and think that his hand has been weakened by his closest ally, Bush, who has not bothered to update himself. Iraq has been a favourite whipping boy ever since the Gulf war when Saddam Hussein was not gracious enough to allow himself to be toppled to wild applause from Bush senior. Indeed it is questionable whether the effort to get Saddam did not in fact help to place him more firmly in control. This is nothing compared to the damage George Bush has caused by including Iran in his rhetoric. The kindest thing that one can say is that his ignorance of conditions in the world beyond America grows by the hour. He still thinks of Ayatollah Khomeini and his fundamentalist regime. Someone should tell Bush that Khomeini is dead, the firman against Salman Rushdie is non est and there is an awakening in Iran. The elected prime minister, Khatami is making great progress in establishing a more liberal regime. Things are going his way although more slowly than some might wish. Bush's uncalled for comment will have the effect of weakening Khatami's hand and there may well be a flood of sentiment against him for not adopting a harder line against America. Khatami has enemies; Bush has strengthened them. Is Bush seeking more enemies or is he merely a danger to America's interests and seeking to keep up hysteria for domestic purposes. Never before has an American President appeared more cocky and abrasive with so little cause. Or has the failure to nab Osama bin Laden and Mullah Omar so affected him that he must get into his cowboy suit again!

At the painful pace at which Bush is displaying any capacity to learn, it will take time for it to sink in that Osama and Mullah Omar are in hiding in Pakistan with several thousand Al Qaeda fighters, protected by Musharraf and the ISI. No wonder Pakistan is not yet declared a terrorist state; if it is to be a long run the retort must be that in the long run we are all dead. Bush made his feelings clear. He talked of those who inhabit his alliance against terrorism standing together and Pakistan is a member of this alliance—hence does not fit into any definition in Bush's Thesaurus on Terrorism.

Bush's thoughtless comment has surprised his friends; British Foreign Secretary Jack Straw is in Washington post haste to see how the damage can be limited and Europe is shattered. There can be no doubt that Bush means well but the attitude that—My friends can do no wrong and the wretched neutrals are suspect till they come cap in hand to Washington—is a dangerous form of jingoism.

2 February 2002

USA, Iraq & Iran

Powell covers up for Bush's outburst

Assuring the world that America was not looking for war, Secretary of State Colin Powell would only say that America "consults its friends and allies before they embark on an adventure". Contrariwise Secretary Rumsfeld manning the Defence Department insists in the context of possibly attacking Iran, that "we do not announce things we are going to do before we do them." Clubbing these and other comments made by important functionaries of the Bush administration on American television networks, it would seem that Iran's fault is two fold—it 'might'—they are not sure—have (a) allowed transit through Iran to Al Qaida and Taliban fighters and did not do what Pakistanis have done, put troops on the border to prevent terrorists from escaping; (b) in other respects not shared Pakistan's stand in fully supporting American action in Afghanistan. If there are other reasons, they have not been disclosed. As for Iraq, the second in the trilogy of Bush's axis of evil, reliable reports from Jerusalem predict that America will attack Saddam Hussein in May, while Powell assures that "America won't go it alone in Iraq". No word yet as to what is to be done to North Korea, the third leg of Bush's trilogy. Why Iran should be faulted for not copying Pakistan in hoodwinking the USA, with malice afore-thought, is not explained. American television networks and leading American newspapers have established the following, also confirmed by reputed American spokesmen. Pakistan has fought alongside Taliban in battalion and brigade strength in Afghanistan, Pakistani military officials, retired and in service, commanded Taliban formations. These Pakistanis were escorted out from Kunduz to Peshawar with American approval at Musharraf's urging with America providing secure air corridors for unspecified sorties. Unfortunately, several thousand key Al Qaida and Taliban elements have, with Pakistani connivance, flown out with them and the presumption is that Osama bin Laden and Mullah Omar are thus currently in PoK and the Baluchistan province of Pakistan. Up to 30,000 American soldiers are in Pakistan to secure Musharraf's compliance with further American demands, as well as to protect him against accidents!

Have Americans been so unnerved by the first direct assault on American soil that it has affected their judgment? Iran is to be attacked because they 'may' have allowed Al Qaida and Taliban terrorists to pass through while undisputed Pakistani involvement in training and leading Taliban terrorists, fighting alongside them and facilitating their shelter within Pakistan, however unwit-tingly as far as America is concerned, is not to be men-tioned because Musharraf is a friend and pressing him further may endanger him! Meanwhile attention is to be diverted towards forging a brand new alliance against Iraq because Saddam has not proved that he is not manufacturing weapons of mass destruction. How he is to prove a negative is not America's concern. Is Iran to be punished for not falling in line with Pakistan? Is the objective to make Sunni Pakistan prevail over Shia Iran and if so what American interests are thus served? Or is the more durable American interest, Iranian oil? Ditto for Iraqi oil? A great deal does not fit. Either America is trying to divert attention from not going after Osama and Omar in Pakistan, or does it want to establish a permanent base in the region. This fear is already driving Russia, China and India into forging a new relationship beyond mere friendship. This is a public position, publicly taken.

Can we return the compliment to Washington and advice 'restraint and calm'!

5 February 2002

Problem of Bush!

Unacceptable security policy

An extreme form of irresponsibility is evident in the new security policy being formulated in the White House. Secretary of State Colin Powell has struggled valiantly to hedge it in with conditions and used a form of words intended to make it appear worthy of serious consideration but unalloyed lunacy is contained in the version articulated by President Bush. To his uncomplicated mind he is justified in wanting to get rid of Saddam Hussein on suspicion of the criminal intent he is assumed to harbour of continuing to defy the United States. Bush wants him to die, to abdicate and leave Iraq, or arrange matters in some other way to make himself scarce and cease irritating the President of the United States. The absence of any credible evidence that Saddam is manufacturing weapons of mass destruction is wholly beside the point and apparently not an obstacle. Bush's solution is to put forward a doctrine which would make Ronald Reagan blush. The United States, he holds, is justified in launching what is euphemistically described as a pre-emptive strike on Iraq on Bush's subjective satisfaction that failure to strike first will result in Saddam striking later.

It is amazing that a country like the United States, which has given the world the First Amendment rights of a free press and helped evolve doctrines adopted by the civilised world of human worth and human personality, should allow its President to so forget himself as to make his country a laughing stock before the international community. In the Bush jurisprudence, suspicion is evidence and accusation equal to guilt. Does it occur to President Bush and if it does not, it should occur to his administration that what the United States does today, some countries will be tempted to do tomorrow. What would George W Bush say if, on a parity of reasoning, Delhi suspects that Musharraf is stockpiling nuclear weapons and jumps to the conclusion that this is enough for a pre-emptive strike against Islamabad! First, and by force of habit, Bush Jr will counsel 'restraint'. Next he will send Armitage here, to be followed by Rumsfeld and if necessary, by Colin Powell. So far we have been spared a dissertation of what it would take to get George Bush himself down here. It would help to know so that we can note what contingency to avoid like the plague.

Get out of the Kyoto protocol, rekindle interest in the star wars of Reagan, knock about other countries economically if they interfere with short-term American interests, this is the stuff of Bush's contribution to human progress. As for his much-trumpeted world war on terrorism, Bush is deaf and blind, both. He will not see that Al Qaida is active in Pakistan; its leaders are protected species there by courtesy of the Pakistani President, who is trusted beyond his capacity to deliver.

Musharraf is not able to rein in the Al Qaida fighters and their leaders and his dilemma is real, although it does not stop him from assuring Bush to the contrary for very short-term advantage. It is crystal clear that the principal target of Al Qaida remains the United States but Bush takes no notice.

Hopes of getting Bush to understand are receding; the question surfaces what will it take for the truth to sink into the American consciousness and travel to policy-making organisations. On this depends the safety of the world.

19 June 2002

Tilting at Windmills!

The issue is bigger than Bush

Now former President Bill Clinton joins the effort to rein in the free ranging George Bush by insisting that Osama bin Laden be caught first before embarking on the adventure to topple Saddam Hussein. He makes very good sense. In the hysteria generated by Bush, priorities dictated by logic and common sense are ignored. The fact is that Osama killed over three thousand people in New York on 11 September 2001 turning the world on its head, and Bush is on record as wanting him dead or alive. He is alive but free and a bigger threat to America and the rest of the world than Saddam Hussein has ever been. Bush's own Secretary of State, the respected Colin Powell, also holds that the Bush priorities are skewed but he uses more diplomatic language. Congress seeks reassurance; he raves and rants but fails to convince even his Republican colleagues, one of whom deplores publicly the excess of hot air and the shortage of evidence. On 12 September Bush is to try and

Tilting at Windmills!

convince a much more sceptical audience at the United Nations.

The question can be asked why has Bush virtually abandoned Afghanistan, taken Pakistan to his bosom and focussed all his attention and the power of his office on Baghdad. An answer is that the American President is quite unable to see both Osama and Saddam at the same time, so he banishes Osama from his radar screen and finds a new hate figure—Saddam. Those who watched his performance on television to convince Congressional leaders must have wondered at how little he has to say— Saddam has weapons of mass destruction and he must be destroyed. Where are the weapons? Bush's answer is that America must be proactive otherwise Saddam will strike. After a little show of resistance and independent thinking Tony Blair has climbed back into Bush's lap as his pet poodle. The German Chancellor takes Blair to the cleaners for his mendacity. There is no doubt that Britain is out on a limb on this question within the European Union; Bush responds by accusing Germany of being the one who is isolated on the question of Saddam. This is dangerous myopia. Is the stress of the job too much for the limited George? He has been on a month's vacation at his Texas ranch but it has not helped—he has returned more rabid than when he left.

The unreasoning emphasis on Iraq has a rational but unconvincing explanation. It is to hide the failure to nab Osama coupled with the fear that if he is tracked down to Pakistan where he is almost certainly hiding and this becomes public knowledge, Bush will have more egg on his face than is produced on his ranch. Somehow his investment in Musharraf must be seen to bear fruit. If Al Qaeda strikes again, Bush has by now prepared the ground for blaming it on Saddam. Inspired stories have begun to appear in the predictable sections of the international media that there is a connection between Saddam and Osama; weren't there some dark reports of Al Qaeda men whom no one has seen, being spotted in Baghdad by people not identified? It is a surprise that the reports are not more specific like Osama being entertained by Saddam to dinner at his palace.

The intellectual abilities of the President of the United States are the butt of jokes and they do have a basis in fact but it has gone beyond a joke. What is at issue here is the safety of the most powerful democracy in the world and as a logical consequence the peace and comfort of the rest of us.

8 September 2002

Our World Too!

Bush's intervention in Germany backfires

President George W Bush has probably succeeded in influencing the German elections to the Bundestag but not in the manner intended. He probably thought he had only to express his preference for the challenger to the German Chancellor and the voters would dutifully carry Herr Edmund Stoiber to a resounding victory. His instant success in forcing the Justice Minister to resign for comparing him to Hitler in his blind hatred of Saddam Hussein may have encouraged him; somebody in his administration should have been knowledgeable enough to tell him that the resignation had nothing to do with any sense of outrage in Germany that the American President should have been so compared but underlines the determination of the German people to forget Hitler as a bad dream and public opinion will turn against anyone who resurrects the name of the Nazi horror, irrespective of the context in which the reference is made.

If Bush were wise—he is anything but—he would have noticed that the object of his support, Herr Stoiber considered Bush's endorsement an embarrassment and acted accordingly. Whereas, earlier he had endorsed the American position on Iraq and was almost ready to go to war in support, he quickly turned around and made it conditional on Security Council endorsement after Bush's flat-footed intervention. Given his mindset, it is probable that Bush does not know how to account for the rejection of his candidate Stoiber and the victory of Chancellor Gerhard Schroeder by however narrow a margin. It will be recalled that Schroeder was trailing in the opinion polls, the economy was down, public perception was gaining ground that the Chancellor's liberal policy on immigration was hurting domestic employment—over 4 million unemployed. Stoiber was forging ahead and the Chancellor was searching for an issue he could exploit and getting increasingly desperate. Along comes the half-witted President of the United States who has not grasped the fundamental principle that foreign intervention, even perceived intervention tends to be the kiss of death. In the event, if a single judge of the American Supreme Court awarded the presidency to Bush by unjustifiably stopping the recount of crucial votes against Bush, then the President in his turn, has awarded the Chancellor-ship of the Bundestag to the very man he wished to exclude, Gerhard Schroeder.

The lesson is as old as history but Bush is not a student of history; he only understands power play and holds the belief with a missionary zeal that America is God's gift to mankind and the heaven born leader of the United States is destined to lead and it is the business of the rest of the world to follow meekly and in silence. He wanted weapons inspectors to return to Baghdad; Saddam complied. He now says Saddam is lying and wants a Security Council resolution to attack Iraq regardless. He says America has a right to pre-emptive strike to forestall Iraqi terrorism, which no one else has seen, but terrorism practiced by steadfast ally Musharraf is a matter to be solved politically! If Bush had a fleeting familiarity with logic he would know that it is not possible to prove a negative; in other words Saddam cannot prove that he is not lying. Bush probably thinks logic is a variation of Logo toys! This is his private problem; the tragedy is that its consequences will be visited upon the entire world.

There is hope that with the renewed mandate Chancellor Schroeder will strengthen the European voice against the reckless adventure that Bush and Blair threaten to unleash upon the world. It is our world too!

24 September 2002

CAVEAT

Sharing the Spoils?

President Bush seems to have run out of excuses in his reckless pursuit of war against Iraq; his diatribe against Saddam Hussein, complete with facial expressions on television, would do credit to a Shakespearean actor—the overriding emotion is quite clearly hatred. "That guy tried to kill my dad in 1993,", wails Bush in the year 2002. As an argument it is about as convincing as the statement of the VHP *mahamantri* who sought to justify the Gujarat riots because a Muslim nawab ordered 200 cows killed in 1713. Bush's ratings in opinion polls must be causing him considerable disquiet and he must hope that before they dip further, he will be able to unleash his war on Iraq—three air strikes have already happened without cause—and the unthinking *mantra*, my country, right or wrong, will prevail.

Tony Blair is in a considerably worse position. He had shot his bolt ahead of the recent Blackpool Labour party conference, by an unbelievably ham-handed brief of 50 pages to justify an attack on Iraq here and now in America's footsteps. All that can be said about the publication is that it would have been better if it had not been offered. The Foreword by barrister Tony Blair declares that it is based on intelligence gathered by the Joint Intelligence Committee, "which is at the heart of the British Intelligence machinery". If that is so, then this particular heart has long since stopped beating! Having made an absurd claim there is a quick retraction. The material is said to be largely secret; the question can be asked, in that case what is it doing on the Internet? Admitting that it is not easy to gather intelligence inside Iraq, the prime minister wants us to accept nevertheless that "he is satisfied as to its authority". And then we have the ultimate idiocy. "It is clear," says Blair, "that despite sanctions, the policy of containment has not worked … ." As clear as mud! Thereafter without much ado, a rush to the predetermined conclusion—Iraq must be destroyed! The Foreword ends with more bizarre propositions: Iraqi planning is aimed at being battle-ready for weapons of mass destruction at 45 minutes' notice. There is not a shred of evidence to support such a conclusion. Which stopwatch is he using? The phrase—weapons of mass destruction—is so overused that it is identified by an abbreviation, WMD. Blair is convinced that Britain is 'faced with someone who has shown himself capable of using WMD'. He was not even thought of when the Americans dropped not one but two WMD in the shape of nuclear bombs on defenceless Japanese civilians in Hiroshima and Nagasaki. What is his defence for such selective indignation over the use of weapons of mass destruction? Can he be heard to say that he wasn't born then and ex hypothesi, did not witness the horror, so it did not happen? Or is he abandoning his training in logic and the art of argument and adopting the rule of thumb of his friends—heads I am right, tails you are wrong!

Meanwhile the brazen arm-twisting of the United Nations proceeds apace, Bush at one arm, Blair at the other. Security Council resolutions, after the Gulf War were not implemented say the duo, so we must have a brand new one. Each passing day the prospect of a French or Russian or Chinese veto in the Security Council increases. Bush thinks he only has to send emissaries to Paris, Moscow and Beijing for these nations to be overwhelmed by this extreme condescension to withdraw the threat and fall in line. Bush has another guess coming. Across the Atlantic, the opposition to Blair's adventurism, shameless and unthinking in America's shadow is growing within the cabinet, the party and the country. Blair has done a good job of reforming the Labour Party and liberating it from the vice-grip of doctrinaire socialism. New Labour is an achievement by any standards but it seems to have caused a rush of blood to the head and Blair thinks he has only to open his mouth and the party will follow him. Some pied piper he takes himself to be! If apprehension turns to reality, the Conservatives will get a boost beyond their wildest imaginings. Truly, some have greatness thrust upon them!

Iraq continues to run rings round the Bush and Blair pair at the diplomatic game. International opinion is firmly against such reckless adventures. The puzzle wrapped inside an enigma is what is it that makes Blair fit so snugly inside Bush's pocket? Even a baby kangaroo will show himself occasionally from the mother's pouch! Or have the two come to a cosy arrangement over the division of Iraqi oil?

6 October 2002

Retreat from Moscow!

Blair accepts that democracy has triumphed

The system of checks and balances in governance does work in mature democracies. In Britain it works faster than in the United States. Britain has been at it for far longer and is much more experienced. It does not share the hysteria that characterises Americans in the mass. It applies to the attempt of the duo, Bush and Blair, Bush leading, Blair following blindly and unthinkingly, to mount an attack on Iraq on the basis of evidence on which no one would hang a fly. Cracks are beginning to appear in the alliance due entirely to the British prime minister's realisation that he cannot get away with it. Strong and publicly expressed dissenting voices are heard from within cabinet, in the Labour party and in the country. The result is a careful but clearly visible retreat from Moscow. Addressing the concluding session of his party's general conference in Blackpool, Blair at last found the realism that has eluded him these past few days and weeks.

He repeated the threat he saw from Saddam Hussein. He insisted that the Iraqi President should be removed to make the world safe for the Bush/Blair brand of peace in our time. He also insisted that he and his American ally wanted United Nations support in the shape of a resolution, to authorise war if so determined by these two leaders without further reference to the Security Council. But he introduced a new condition, which effectively rolled back the rhetoric of the recent past. He equated the situation in Iraq with that in the Middle East and held that a Palestinian state be declared and that Israel withdraw from all Palestinian areas at once. It was clever of him. For one, he struck a sympathetic chord in Britain's long-standing bias against the Israelis which dates back to the British mandate in Palestine, flouted by Jews to be able to claim a state of their own at the end of World War II. For another he made it impossible for Bush to agree, given the influential Jewish lobby on the east coast of the United States, which no American president can ignore. No doubt Bush told him so in a conversation he held almost immediately after the bombshell exploded in Blackpool.

With Blair retreating from his reckless posture under pressure from his own party and unambiguous public opinion polls, Bush finds the ground rapidly slipping from under him. Blair has made his point and although nobody overheard the conversation it can be assumed that he pointed to the lack of support from the French, the Russians and the Chinese. In this he resembles the Pakistani President Musharraf, who has been telling Bush that if it were not for India he, Musharraf, would be much closer to the American administration. Bush may invite contempt for his lack of intellect, inexperience and without a capacity for discernment but the American establishment does extend beyond the White House.

In the coming weeks and months we can expect to see Blair making it clear that this speech was not a flash in the pan; likewise it is possible that Bush will begin to emphasise other means that he wants to exhaust before going to war even as he continues to berate Saddam. One way and another Saddam Hussein can breathe a little more easily. It is to be hoped that he will be controlled and careful. He is a master of the art and there is no reason to suppose that he will disappoint.

8 October 2002

Bringing up George!

America bows to Security Council

No one should be surprised that the White House has climbed down from its wholly indefensible position over attacking Saddam Hussein and Iraq forthwith, in spite of firm opposition from three of the five permanent members of the Security Council and despite growing opposition reflected in opinion polls within the United States. It was to be expected that George Bush would soldier on, accusing Saddam of holding, or in the alternative preparing to hold, or failing that intending to acquire, the wherewithal for production of what the Americans and the British coyly call—WMD—or weapons of mass destruction. Both went to great lengths to produce dossiers of 'top-secret' evidence against Iraq, ignoring the point that if all this was top secret, what was it doing on the Internet anyway? The stubbornly held American position at the United Nations was to have a single resolution, which would come into force automatically and authorise the use of force, the moment the head of the weapons inspection team reported that Saddam was not cooperating. Not one nation, except the United States had any stomach for such an aberration of international law. Bush has now had to agree that in the event of an adverse report from the weapons inspectors it would be taken to the Security Council and it would be for the Council to proceed further as may be dictated by circumstances at that time.

The last straw that broke the back of the camel called George Bush, was no doubt the change in the position taken by his ally, Tony Blair, who made his continued support for the Bush position conditional upon Israel bring forced to leave all Arab lands occupied since 1967 and declare a Palestinian state simultaneously and forthwith. Bush realised that the game was up only after several days and a telephone conversation with Blair to accept the British position for real. The difficulty with taking extreme and unreasonable positions in international relations is that retreat from them becomes embarrassing and painful. Bush has not had the experience earlier, but he should contemplate how different it would have been if he had heeded the fact that the world extends beyond the landmass between the Atlantic and Pacific oceans and there are other influential decision makers than the occupant of the White House. The decision to bow to the Security Council was therefore more painful than it need have been. George Bush is head of the most powerful nation on earth; it is incongruous that he should behave as he does. It is to be hoped that the immediate lessons to be learnt are at least two in number. One, that going after Saddam on the ground that—'This guy tried to kill my father in 1993'—is, if the conesequences are not so serious, almost laughable. Two, to generalise from the American experience and claim for himself the right of pre-emptive attack merely on unsubstantiated apprehensions even as he specifically denies it to other nations more threatened and actually harmed with malice aforesaid, and dismiss this as a problem to be settled politically, is to bring the Presidency of the United States of America into contempt and ridicule. It was left to Colin Powell to concede that India had a better right in the context of Pakistani terrorism in Kashmir just as it was left to the State Department spokesman to announce that America will, after all, come back to the Security Council if the weapons inspectors report that Saddam is not co-operating.

It all puts one in mind of the enormously popular comic strip whose name could be changed to Bringing up George, from Bringing up Father. It is a sobering thought that if the system of checks and balances did not work in the mature democracies no part of this would be funny.

22 October 2002

International Brigand!

An anachronism in the 21st century

George W Bush, Jr. by fortunate circumstance, President of the United States, is breaking new ground. Forced by international opinion to wait for the weapons inspectors to complete their work in Iraq—Saddam Hussein's response to the latest Security Council Resolution is the first step—he persists in threats of military action because he is convinced that Saddam will not comply, continues to build an assault force in preparation for war, signs appropriations of $200 billion for the war nobody wants and harangues the world to choose between him and Saddam. 'That man tried to kill my Dad in 1993' is the basic premise and justification for hostilities. Bush would be shocked to be compared to Narendra Modi in Gujarat—he too relies on something that is supposed to have happened in the distant past to justify unspeakable horrors unleashed upon a whole community in Gujarat—what some nawab is supposed to have done to 200 cows in 1713 AD!

A look at the relevant timetable is instructive. Saddam was supposed to deliver a detailed list of weapons manufacture and storage facilities in Iraq, by a deadline. Even as the deadline approached, Bush was airing his conviction that Saddam would not comply. He did comply, and within the deadline. On 8 December he produced a dossier of some 12,000 pages. It stands to reason that it would take days for effective and credible verification of the mass of information supplied. But it would take no time at all, if there were a prearranged decision to reject whatever was offered, out of hand. The rejection by the Bush administration of the Iraqi documents as not a full declaration, on the very same date proves, if proof were necessary, that a prearranged decision existed in Washington and London.

There is another aspect to this spectacular and despicable resolve to come to predetermined conclusions, regardless of the evidence. Saddam has been insisting that he holds no prohibited weapons of mass destruction. It is not necessary to take him at his word; his past conduct precludes such trust and confidence. But hence the elaborate inspections procedure adopted by the Security Council. Surely this procedure must first be followed meticulously and fairly. Saddam is being asked to prove a negative. If Bush were to consult lawyers of his choice, and that is taking a risk, he would be told that it is a failure of logic to ask for proof of a negative. The only possibility that can help Bush is that he is in possession of evidence to prove that Saddam has filed an incomplete or incorrect return of the weapons and their capability to the inspectors and the Security Council. If that is so, it is surely for him to prove that Iraq is lying. He is not doing so. Threats and assertions that he is right are utterly inadequate and are no substitute for evidence. Also, it is morally indefensible.

Bush must be told plainly what he is about. He is guilty as charged of bias and prejudice against Iraq and its head of government, Saddam Hussein. In deciding to go to war as he has planned to do all along, brushing side evidence, ignoring the latest Security Council Resolution even as he asks Saddam to submit to it is to sink to a new low in international relations and exhibit vulgarity of a nauseating kind. America right or wrong is suitable for the Klu Klux Klan, it is not an appropriate position to take for the most powerful democracy on earth with a reputation to lose. An international brigand in the twenty-first century is an anachronism that must not be allowed to stand.

10 December 2002

Omissions & Problems!

Perfidy in evaluating Iraq's declaration

George W Bush's tendency to regard his own bias and prejudices over Iraq including his preoccupation with Saddam Hussein, as a substitute for world opinion continues unabated. The latest to fall victim to the high-pressure salesmanship seems to be Hans Blix, the Chief Weapons Inspector of the UN team who is said, by the Americans to be preparing to get into line—it has been announced that his report to the Security Council on Thursday will strengthen the US position. The White House spokesman Ari Fleischer is already expressing the President's concern about omissions and problems in the Iraqi declaration and laying down the deadline as end January for a decision on peace or war. We can be assured that it will be war, if Bush is allowed to rush headlong into it as he plans to do. As regards what the 'omissions and problems' are, we are not allowed to know except the old fallacious line that Saddam has not yet proved the negative that he has not yet made a full declaration of the weapons he had at the start of the Gulf war.

Nerves in international relations are getting frayed and the world economy, already in crisis, is showing all the signs that war is inevitable. The price of gold has touched a new high, oil prices are rising, coupled with rumours that Saddam Hussein is planning a scorched earth policy, setting fire to and destroying his oil fields and will attempt to release biological and chemical weapons. Largely attended meetings billed as those of Iraqi dissidents are held, no doubt the Americans are organising them to the amusement of Saddam who knows what value to put on these gatherings intended to soak up American dollars and making noises that would be music to Bush's ears. Then an extraordinary demand has been made; that Saddam hand over or let go Iraqi scientists to be named by the Americans, with their families who would be transported outside Iraq and encouraged to make noises about Saddam's perfidy which will, without further ceremony, be treated as sworn testimony against the Iraqi dictator. What will happen to them after they have perjured themselves as tutored and have been duly paid off is not known. There is no suggestion that the Americans will retain an interest in them after their purpose has been served—Saddam can go after them for all that Washington cares. Who in these circumstances will come forward and perform is difficult to tell, it partly depends on whether the payoff is large enough for them to make their life elsewhere in the world, assuming that any country is willing to risk a Saddam operation to get them on their land.

The British are under the impression that they exercise an influence on Bush and will prevail. One would hope so but London must understand that they are dealing with a new phenomenon in the world, a new and frightening version of the closed mind, comparable to that open-minded public performer Osama bin Laden. Bush will hear no voice but his own and his administration conveys to him that no other voice is relevant. Even the candid admission by North Korea that they are in brazen breach of agreements entered into with America, Japan and South Korea to cease and desist from going ahead with their nuclear programme in return for two nuclear power plants for civilian use. Both sides are in breach but that does not help. The problem created is urgent and fraught with grave peril but Bush cannot deal with North Korea and Saddam at the same time; he has limitations! The Security Council is being hijacked, the UN Secretary-General must wait in queue to be heard by Bush and there is no one to disperse the war clouds gathering ominously. At this point at any rate, the checks and balances in the governance of the United States do not appear to work. They must begin before it is too late.

21 December 2002

Dangerous Politician!

George Bush earns the epithet

As the year draws to a close, the world's attention is focused, uneasily indeed, on what the Nobel Prize winning writer, Günter Grass calls a 'truly dangerous politician', George W Bush. As far as President Bush is concerned, Iraq can do nothing right. He wanted arms inspectors to return to Iraq; they did. He wanted them armed with the mandate to visit any site, any time, often and without notice; Saddam Hussein complied. He demanded a full dossier of Iraq's weapons stockpile and capacity by a deadline: Iraq produced it with a day to spare. The 1,200 page document was to be presented to the head of the inspection team, Hans Blix, who was to deliver a considered evaluation to members of the Council. Bush's storm-troopers ambush the document on its way to Blix, without a 'please' or 'by your leave', saying they would examine it first. The same day, and it can be no one's case that there was time for even a cursory reading, Bush's Defence Secretary brands the document a rehash of old material and declares it incomplete. He also forecasts that Blix's report to the Security Council days later would support the American position. Is Donald Rumsfeld a clairvoyant or merely delivering a predetermined verdict?

They next want a list of Iraqi scientists who may have worked on nuclear and allied research; 500 names are provided without delay. What is Bush's response? His New Year resolution has an attack on Iraq on top of his agenda, exposing his motives, his disregard for evidence—even Blix asks that his inspectors be given more time to do their work—and confirming that he suffers from that most distressing of human afflictions—a closed mind. The Secretary-General of the UN, Kofi Annan, makes the same plea for time but Bush is both blind and deaf. The Inspectors are working hard. They are into the second month of their work, they have not been obstructed and they have found nothing. Bush goes on to claim a broad coalition against Iraq; it is so broad that it falls flat. Apart from Tony Blair whose motives are thoroughly questionable, the only other country, Qatar is cajoled, bribed, threatened and taken for granted by an aggressive America to provide bases for the attack on Iraq.

With an exquisite sense of timing Kim Jong-II of North Korea cocks a snook at America, breaking locks to resume building nuclear facilities and sending inspectors from the IAEA in Vienna packing, knowing that Bush cannot fight on two fronts, despite Rumsfeld's threat to do just that. North Korea sees no sense in a nuclear war, it has no targets, its relations with the South are excellent—the country is starving and its economy is in a shambles. Its hope is to frighten America and Bush into loosening their purse strings; it wants to replicate what Musharraf has accomplished—$4 billion in two lots already under the belt and immunity from scrutiny of its terrorist activities. Kim knows that American concern for terrorism is selective and to that extent hypocritical. He wants to take similar advantage. LK Advani is therefore right to send a strong and clear warning to the international community (read Bush) to take note that the epicentre of terrorist activity has shifted from Afghanistan to Pakistan.

Bush must know or must be told that he may have succeeded in whipping America into a dangerous hysteria but his antics have ensured that Osama bin Laden has yielded place to—guess who—at the top of the World's table of the most dangerous man on earth—George W Bush, by unfortunate intervention of a Supreme Court justice, President of the United States of America.

Have a Happy New Year!

31 December 2002

Powell Tries Hard!

No compelling case on Iraq

The presentation by Secretary of State Colin Powell of the American case against Iraq to the Security Council was sober, professional and was as persuasive as he could make it in terms of style and tone but it made no compelling case. Indeed the effort, thinly disguised, was to have something for everyone. The Russians were tempted with a link between Iraq and Chechen rebels who are causing President Putin such headaches, links between Al Queda and Iraq were sought to be established by alleging that some Al Queda operative had spent an unspecified amount of time in Baghdad and could not have failed to meet Saddam Hussein. The French were complimented for apprehending some suspicious characters in Paris and gently warned that the threat would not recede until Saddam Hussein was sent into exile. The Chinese have a problem with Islamic fundamentalism, which Powell did not fail to exploit. Saddam was held to be hiding weapons of mass destruction because he was mixing 18 trucks capable of carrying prohibited weapons among thousands of normal vehicles and it was held to be axiomatic that it was beyond the ability of the weapons inspectors to pick these 18 out of the rest. There were a lot of satellite pictures, but it needed American labels to tell us what they were being used for; there was no independent verification. Generally, dates were peppered about to make allegations but most of them go back to before the Gulf War.

Violation of human rights was pleaded forgetting that this was not the subject of the proceedings; that Saddam Hussein is alleged to have killed thousands of his own people, especially the Kurds, was more suited to proceedings before the International Court of Justice. The effect was irresistible that everything in sight and other charges not visible were being hurled against Iraq in the hope that something would stick. Not an object lesson in the art of argument but pressure from the paranoid Bush was palpable. The Americans could not be pleased that as Colin Powell finished his marathon performance—some 75 minutes—the Chinese, the French and the Russians unequivocally pleaded for sufficient time to be given to the UN weapons inspectors to complete their work and all three have a veto in the Security Council. All that can be said for Powell's effort was that it was more bearable than the rabble rousing and emotional approach to which, we have been treated repeatedly in the past, by George W Bush, President of the United States of America.

Never before has evidence and argument been held hostage to a single country's obsessions, more correctly a single individual's paranoia, aided and abetted by a small coterie of advisors who have made up their minds that war is the way to gain access to Iraqi oil, to lebensraum in the Iraqi desert for the hapless Palestinians and perhaps significant in its own way, to thoughts of vengeance for having tried, so we are told, to kill the President's father. There is no real proof for any of these assumptions but they are plausible and the alternative is to conclude that the American President needs treatment to wash out the poison he has imbibed without anyone's encouragement —unlike the pitiable youth who committed suicide in full view of others who egged him on for no better reason than to watch him die—assuming that advances in medical science are sufficient to help provide a solution.

Of course a dramatic improvement in the President's condition can come about from another but potent source —if the popularity ratings fall below acceptable levels— they are moving that way already!

7 February 2003

CAVEAT

Destination Disaster!

The reckless disregard, even contempt for compelling arguments for America to hold its hand, which George Bush displays simply because they do not fit in with his resolve to attack Iraq and enforce a 'regime change' in Baghdad, represents a new low in international relations. Since Secretary of State Colin Powell's first command performance in the Security Council, which conspicuously failed to shake the Council and the world beyond, Bush has had to stomach fresh humiliation.

Tony Blair utterly failed to move President Chirac, despite trying to add personal chemistry to lack of reason and argument. As soon as Powell had finished, France, Russia and China took the floor and stressed that weapons inspectors must be given the time they needed to complete their task. Pakistan, a client state, added its voice against the aggression proposed. Sensing frustration in the Security Council, Bush turns to Nato. Three prominent members, France, Germany and Belgium, meet within the Nato framework and resolve to oppose any attack on Iraq, whatever the subterfuge employed. Bush accuses them of dividing Nato; a classic instance of the pot calling the kettle black! The USA wants bases in Turkey to launch attacks on Iraq and this is bound to invite retaliation. Hapless Turkey has failed to obtain assurances in terms of a binding provision in the Nato Charter for member nations to come to the aid of any of them if attacked. France, Germany and Belgium are clear that inviting an attack is not a contingency covered by the Charter.

Meanwhile, the megalomaniac Bush continues with vitriolic assaults warning Saddam Hussein that the game is over. The only game being played, and it is a dangerous game, originates in the White House. President Chirac, the experienced statesman, flatly contradicts Bush by declaring that 'Iraq is not a game'. Unbelievable but true is the report that Bush's National Security Advisor, Condoleezza Rice, sought out the Chief Weapons Inspector and pressed him, in his second report, to find Saddam Hussein in 'material breach' of obligations. It passes belief that a senior official of Bush's administration should so forget herself as to lobby Hans Blix in this brazen fashion. I suppose she does not forget herself; she merely remembers what Bush wants. This is not pressure; it is several steps into the realm of lunacy.

In the event, Blix reported on Friday that Iraq was cooperating, and although he still had a few questions, he was confident that to continue with inspections was the way forward. Several other countries led by France made forceful supporting noises. The Security Council is, however, hanging on the edge of a precipice with Powell advocating closure of debate and war, although he avoided the word, but Bush addressing a domestic audience, abused the Security Council and the United Nations for their inaction, in the manner to which he is now firmly addicted.

Comic relief comes in the shape of the VHP's own Pravin Togadia scrambling to Bush's side for no better reason than that Iraq is a Muslim state. Join America he cries, this is the way to profit from Iraq's discomfiture! He even puts a figure on it, upwards of $120 million. On a parity of reasoning, he must, needs defend Pervez Musharraf who fell in line with Bush for two dollops of $2 billion each! What a clumsy negotiator is Togadia! At least Musharraf played coy and waited to be wooed. Togadia rushes in for a mess of pottage! The crowning irony, which Bush is unable to see is that while he brushes aside all evidence, including weapons inspection reports, simply because they are inconvenient, he continues to counsel India and Pakistan to start a dialogue at once, for according to this one man threat to world peace, it is the way ordained. He has no answer when the Indian External Affairs Minister contemptuously retorts that he is waiting for Bush to open a dialogue with Osama bin Laden!

Bush has taken to bad-mouthing Saddam for being a dictator. If it were not a waste of time, I should like to ask Bush whether steadfast ally Pervez Musharraf is a dyed-in-the-wool liberal and democrat! When senior American officials came calling the other day to justify blind support to Musharraf despite damning evidence that he was shielding Osama and Omar in Pakistan and fomenting terrorism, their defence was that otherwise Musharraf would be in danger. I asked where they got authority to decide who governs Pakistan? I warned that unthinking support to Musharraf would be the kiss of death for their steadfast ally. Before a Senate Committee, a ranking official of Bush's administration now deposes that risk of a coup or assassination is a real danger and it would 'result in an extremist Pakistan'. Somebody is confusing cause and effect here! Osama is alive, courtesy Bush and Musharraf, and is not wasting his time. If these officials have reported back accurately, they can wallow in the knowledge that they have brought it upon themselves by their mindless policy on Pakistan. I told them so!

Truly, none so blind as those that will not see and none so deaf as those that will not hear!

16 February 2003

Tottering on the Brink

Saddam upsets calculations

The order of the Chief Weapons Inspector Hans Blix to the Iraqi authorities to start destroying Al Samoud missiles together with their engines, warheads, guidance and control systems, with effect from 1 March, gives some indication of the pressure under which the poor weapons inspectors are working in Iraq. The point to be made at the threshold is that the inspection team derives its authority from the Security Council and is mandated to report to the Council; this has happened twice already. It is no part of the responsibility of the team to issue orders to the Iraqi authorities to destroy any particular weapons system. It follows that if the finding that the missiles are capable of a range beyond the limit laid down had been reported to the Council, Iraq would have had an opportunity of rebuttal and it would have been for the Council to consider both sets of representations and come to a decision. Instead Blix has been pressured to act as inspector, advocate, judge and executioner, all rolled into one. Somebody should point out to the Security Council that there has been a grave miscarriage of justice here.

The point being missed is that for the past many weeks, George W Bush has made no secret of his desire to go to war against Iraq; efforts to bully the French, the Germans, the Russians and the Chinese, not to speak of the Turks, by a not so subtle mix of threats and blandishments could not have escaped notice. Verbal assaults in the Security Council asking for war to the accompaniment of attacks from the air over Iraq have become commonplace—the Americans are furious that Iraq is not patiently accepting the punishment meted out. Under such constant threats and pressures is it reasonable to expect that Saddam Hussein should deny himself his only means of defense, the ability to retaliate and make life a little uncomfortable for his tormentors? By proxy, George Bush is asking Saddam to put up his gloves and accept any punishment he chooses to dole out and not resist raining death and destruction on a defenceless population. No wonder Saddam has rejected the demand to destroy the missiles.

Bush's pet poodle, Tony Blair, is adding his voice to the din created by the Americans by laying down deadlines for war—mid-March—has he not heard of the ides of March! According to the Bush/Blair plan here is proof that Saddam refuses to be destroyed and that is reason enough for the votaries of freedom, due process and democracy to start a war and divide up Iraqi oil reserves. Saddam is no angel but there is something heroic about his retort to debate the issue with Bush. The encounter between the greenhorn Bush and the vastly experienced Saddam would have been a treat to watch if the consequences were not so serious. The obvious next step is to go to war but the sheer audacity of Saddam Hussein has done two things—one it has vastly increased his presence in the Muslim world and among those accustomed to think for themselves. The unexpected challenge from Saddam may well induce rethinking in Washington along the lines that Saddam may have other weapons up his sleeve, which may dramatically upset calculations and force consideration of body bags arriving in the United States—a contingency that must induce a pause in plans. For the peace and sanity of the world, it is a possibility devoutly to be wished.

26 February 2003

Bush's Frustration

Blix Report checkmates America

The Chief Weapons Inspector for Iraq, appointed by the Security Council, Hans Blix, reports that Baghdad is carrying out substantial disarmament and there is no proof of hiding banned weapons in mobile laboratories. Irked by the insistence of the United States to use any pretext to justify war and force a change of guard upon Iraq, Blix says—"we are not watching the destruction of toothpicks". The UN atomic energy chief, El Baradei echoes Blix—inspections have revealed no sign of any prohibited activity. A substantial number of missiles have been destroyed and the programme is for real. Clearly the inspections are working and Bush has come to realize, however reluctantly, that his plan to wreak death and destruction on Baghdad for no better reason than 'trying to kill my Dad in 1993' is making him the laughing stock of the world. Colin Powell, trying to reiterate Bush's position by debunking whatever Blix and El Baradei are saying only invites pity; his feeling that he should stay in the Administration for whatever sobering effect he can provide on his boss may be true but there are limits beyond which it is difficult to make excuses for a fine soldier and Secretary of State.

Tony Blair claims credit for holding Bush in check for as long as he has but here too there are limits. A third of his Parliamentary Party is in revolt; his effort to portray himself as some kind of latter day Winston Churchill standing firm, promising only blood, toil, tears and sweat, is not getting off the ground and he is left with no alternative but to point out to Bush how it would look if Germany, France and Russia between them cast three vetoes where one would suffice to stop the megalomaniac President of the United States in his tracks.

The pressure on Turkey to provide bases to make an attack on Iraq both convenient and cheap can be imagined. Thirty billion dollars in guarantees and another ten billion dollars in cash here and now is not chicken feed. Accustomed to get his way, Bush must wonder what manner of men are Turks who resist such a fortune and prefer to stand aloof. For a man accustomed to believe that what is good for America is, ex-hypothesi, good for the world, coupled with the belief held with a religious faith that everything and everyone has a price, it must be a shattering blow to his pride. And yet it is better that Bush's pride be hurt rather than watch the world plunge into unimagined chaos and destruction.

The cold calculation in Bush's plans must not be missed. There is first the problem of re-election. A quick ruthless war with ten times the destruction in the first day than was caused in the entire Gulf war, as Bush has threatened is cheap at the price to ensure another four years. Besides there will be plenty of cheap oil for his Texan friends who have invested so heavily in him. Then there is the lunatic fringe, which wants the Iraqi desert to populate surplus Palestinians and ease the pressure on Israel. Whatever the motive, it is clear that it is unworthy. It is not the business of the world to come to the aid of George Bush.

9 March 2003

CAVEAT

On a Razor's Edge!

History repeats itself because no one learns the lessons of history. Let me go back to the end of the First World War. In 1918 the victorious allies imposed very harsh conditions on Germany's Weimar Republic and generated such resentment and despair that Hitler emerged as an answer to a defeated nation's injured pride. In 1945 after World War II, lessons were indeed learnt. Japan and Germany were treated magnanimously and helped to come into their own, thanks largely to the United States and the Marshall Plan named after Secretary of State, George Marshall, a statesman of high calibre and vision. There was also the need to build a front against communism, threatening to overpower the world, but this takes nothing away from the credit due to what was the free world led by the United States.

What we are witnessing today is a diminution of the American dream, an abandonment of the great liberal values of democracy established by leaders of the calibre of Franklin Roosevelt, revered justices of the Supreme Court who enunciated and entrenched those values in the American consciousness like Learned Hands, Felix Frankfurter, Louis Brandeis. They were an inspiration wherever democracy lived and liberty thrived. In St Xavier's College and Government Law College, Bombay we imbibed the words of Britain's Alexander Pope:

> Ain't please Your Honour,
> quoth the peasant,
> T'is same dessert is not
> so pleasant!
> Give me back my hollow tree
> A crust of bread and Liberty!

We quoted Latin–*Ubi Libertas; ibi patria*! (Where Liberty dwells there is my country!)

The slide back began in the early nineties with the Gulf War following Iraq's invasion of Kuwait. The lessons learnt began to dim. Hatred, vengeance, greed and worse took root. Humiliating sanctions imposed on a defeated Iraq included limits on exploiting their oil; ridiculously restricted quantities are allowed; half the sales proceeds can be utilised in a controlled manner for food, medicines and suchlike, but the other half is spent on making sure that Saddam Hussein is not a threat to his neighbours again. Fair enough, but sanctions have lasted over a decade and caused horrendous hardships; punishment has long ceased to fit the crime. And while we are about crime and punishment and the need to destroy weapons of mass destruction, it bears recall that the only nation ever to use nuclear weapons unhesitatingly against defenceless civilians, not once but twice, is the United States. Limiting American casualties in war is not an acceptable excuse. And now, to intimidate Saddam, no angel by any means, America boasts of having developed the mother of all bombs, all 21,000 pounds of it!

Under President George Bush, in office by decision of a single justice of the Supreme Court appointed by his father, America has become unrecognisable. It is probing depths to see how low it can sink in the esteem of the world. The entire edifice of the United Nations is in mortal danger. The will of the international community is brashly flouted. Bush proclaims that those not with him are against him! He wants to wreak vengeance on Saddam because 'that guy tried to kill my Dad'. Bush senior wants his son to leave open a line of retreat from untenable positions; George W responds by burning all bridges behind him. Carefully calibrated rules of procedure in the UN are ignored. Three permanent members of the Security Council have threatened to use their vetoes; one is enough to block any resolution. Bush cannot muster even a simple majority of nine votes; if he gets it by his unique methods of persuasion, he will declare a veto counts for nothing. If he fails he will say he did not need another resolution anyway! 'Bushism' has entered the *Oxford English Dictionary*. If you want synonyms, here they are—Fascism, Hitlerism. His pet poodle, Tony Blair faces a revolt within his own Labour Party. Defence Secretary Rumsfeld's way of helping Blair is to publicly doubt whether he will be allowed to join America in attacking Iraq; his remedy—let Britain keep out, America will rely on a new formation—'an international coalition'—a respectable phrase for a despicable grouping eyeing Iraqi oil reserves. Proof lies in Rumsfeld's threat to exclude Britain from any part in rebuilding Iraq, meaning no share in lucrative contracts and in dividing up the oil. He retracts but it is too late. Blair reads the message correctly and insists he will deliver. Such determination is worthy of a better cause than aggrandisement.

I am put in mind of Lewis Carroll's quaint rhyme:
>The time has come, the Walrus said, to talk
>of many things;
>Of shoes and ships and sealing wax: Of
>cabbages and Kings.
>And why the sea is burning hot and
>whether pigs have wings!

Pigs don't have wings even in America but it is time to tell the Walrus in the White House that the time has come to talk!

16 March 2003

Tony's Goose Cooked!

Blair risks future for a mess of pottage

George Bush is reduced to forcing Turkey's hand, begging Australia for 2,000 troops and shopping around in Poland, Denmark and wherever else he can get symbolic gestures of support for his vendetta against Iraq and Saddam Hussein. Turkey has postponed a second vote and limited it to use of its airspace. The Danish prime minister has had paint splashed over him and Australia's John Howard has been barricaded in his residence. Spain's prime minister faced hostile demonstrations including banners inside Parliament and had to promise to limit involvement to humanitarian assistance. Bush tried to get a simple majority in the Security Council for a questionable resolution to cover the premeditated attack on Iraq without risking American lives. Never has the world faced such blatant contempt for International Law, put in place with significant contributions from the self-same United States, but trampled underfoot by a President who listens to nothing but the sound of his own voice. The vultures gathering for the kill at his bidding have, by their conduct, raised Saddam Hussein to the level of a legend in his lifetime. It was not an edifying spectacle to see a grim British Ambassador to the United Nations admit to the failure of the attempt to get a face-saving bare majority in the Security Council and pretend that a veto from France and Germany counts for nothing. The setback exposes the international bandits as nothing else could have done. All honour to France and Germany for standing firm against the attempted rape of the UN, with Russia threatening cancellation of a pact with the US to reduce nuclear stockpiles. All seem to have told Bush what he can do with his dollars.

Tony Blair must be very confident of his share in the spoils, with which he hopes to silence leaders of stature in his own party. The standing ovation that greeted Robin Cook when he announced his resignation from Blair's government should alert him to what is in store. He can reflect that depending on Conservatives to come to his aid after the revolt of over a hundred of his own MPs, will prove to be the kiss of death for the party he did so much to revive after the disastrous socialist era. He fails to see that he is shooting himself in the foot, nay both feet! The credit, if it can be called that, for the Commons vote to follow America will be claimed by the Conservatives, America's traditional friends, while his own party will split down the middle and get lost in the wilderness.

Surely Bush has struck rock bottom with his speech to the American people. Accusing Saddam of all possible evils, against America, against his neighbours, against the world, he thought up a new one—Saddam is running 'rape houses'. Even those few Iraqis who are cosying up to Bush for what they think they can get out of it, have not thought of that! After his performance Bush sought to

Tony's Goose Cooked!

portray himself as firm, resolute, in complete command of himself and sure of his nation's support. He played with his dogs on the White House lawns! He may well get the support, given the level of hysteria he has whipped up. But by the same token, it will evaporate without a trace if his plans go awry and body bags begin to arrive at American airports. What is right and wrong has long ceased to count.

20 March 2003

CAVEAT

Bush's Grubby War!

T he game plan should be clear. The people of Iraq who will run the country after Saddam, will give long-term contracts ... for oil exploration to American and British companies. The war for democracy, justice and peace on earth and goodwill to men, particularly Iraqis, unleashed by self-righteous leaders in America and Britain began inauspiciously with a *faux pas*, which left egg on the face of the American President. Early morning on day one, the CIA Director tells Bush he spies a concentration of Iraqi leaders including Saddam Hussein and knows where they are heading—he seeks instructions. Bush emerges from a three-hour huddle with his National Security Council and gives orders for what, in effect, is a sneak assassination attempt. It badly misfires. The British say it was a warning shot across the bows; Americans, less circumspect, call it a 'target of opportunity' to decapitate the top Iraqi leadership! Both headquarters in Qatar are within hailing distance but coordination seems lacking. So there we have it; the great coalition of the willing, in Bush's trite phrase, failing its first propaganda skirmish.

Saddam retaliates with missiles into Kuwait and has the satisfaction of having American and British troops reach for their gas masks—repeatedly. Prime Minister Tony Blair meets journalists outside Downing Street, to be told that he is at war. Foreign Secretary Jack Straw is yanked out of bed to be given the message. Is Bush taking Britain for granted? Later Blair leaves for Europe, on a damage control exercise, and returns empty-handed. Chasms have deepened. Condemnation and massive protests in the streets are everywhere and growing by the hour.

Blair's denunciation of Saddam includes blaming him for Iraqi women and children dying of neglect. He misses the point. This is a direct consequence of sanctions for prolonging which he and Bush are primarily responsible. He promises that after Saddam, Iraq's oil revenues will "be held in a UN-administered trust for the benefit of the Iraqi people". If the Oil for Food Programme now halted is any guide, half the proceeds were spent on weapons inspectors and other measures to control Iraq. The game plan should be clear. 'The people of Iraq' who will run the country after Saddam, will give long-term contracts—30 to 50 years—for oil exploration to American and British companies and the skewed agreements will not permit any amendments. Bush, Cheney and Rumsfeld are all experienced oilmen and know how to operate. Also, the reconstruction contracts, readied by USAID, have two clauses—'buy American' and 'anti-abortion'. If Britain allows abortion, Blair's contractors have a problem. The slip is showing badly. It is also plain how disinterested is American and British concern for Iraq's reconstruction.

There is another difficulty. The 1991 Gulf war was funded largely by Saudi Arabia. There is no hope of a repeat. Europe is alienated and will refuse to contribute to repair damage inflicted against its will. If America is left to foot the bill, its promises will be as reliable as those to reconstruct Afghanistan. Meantime, bodybags of personnel are already on their way to the US and the UK.

Turkey will only allow overflights for American aircraft. Its army has its own agenda in northern Iraq, its own targets of opportunity, which do not necessarily square with American plans. The move into southern Iraq, inhabited by Shias who hate Saddam, has been halted for a while. After two days of waiting for Saddam to raise the white flag, Bush unleashes a blitzkrieg on Baghdad. Loud protests are bound to get louder. The sight of a bully posing as freedom fighter is nauseating. Also, as Russian President Putin rightly warns, terrorism will intensify on his doorstep in Chechnya and around the world. Ironically, Americans everywhere will face greater danger then ever before.

George Bush's performance from the Oval Office would do credit to a preacher of some obscure cult, unconscious of contradictions mouthed, with faith in his spurious righteousness. Such men sleep soundly; in their spare time, they play with their dogs! With what face can Bush accuse Saddam of lack of decency and morality and a disdain for civilian casualties? He also touts a coalition of thirty-five countries; that is the lie direct. He includes those who limit their gestures to permit overflights, humanitarian assistance and other tokens to placate an unbalanced Bush. And while he insists it is a coalition effort, he claims –'On my orders' the war has begun.

The will of the UN is shamelessly flouted. Foreign Secretary Jack Straw, a barrister by training, argues that Resolution 1441 already provides for the use of force if Iraq does not comply. If that is so, why did Britain try so hard to get another resolution? France, Germany, Russia and China have lectured Britain and America on the illegality of their action. Their reply—our lawyers say it is legal! Some lawyers, some law! There is outrage everywhere and not only in the Muslim world. Regimes in Saudi Arabia and its neighbourhood and in Pakistan are in real danger as they are seen as supporting America. It is inconceivable that a man so limited in intellect can single-handedly change the world—for the worse and so quickly!

23 March 2003

CAVEAT

Bush's Law!

Having appointed the weapons inspectors and set up the machinery for their work, it is the legal responsibility and prerogative of the same Security Council to decide when to withdraw them.

The final idiocy...is for Bush to threaten to take Saddam to the International Criminal Court to stand trial for war crimes even as America refuses to sign the convention setting up the Court and does not accept its jurisdiction!

It is claimed that George Bush, and constant ally Tony Blair, have consulted lawyers and were advised that their unprovoked attack on Iraq—mere suspicions are not provocation—was legal. I would like to see the Case for Opinion submitted and the name of the lawyers in question! One reason publicly given is— Saddam 'tried to kill my Dad in 1993'. For Bush to treat this as the base for policy or even trot it out as an excuse to go to war is to expose himself to the contempt and ridicule of the world. The other reason stems from the outright refusal of America and Britain to accept the several reports of the weapons inspectors appointed by the Security Council that no weapons of mass destruction had been found despite the most anxious search. Inspectors were careful to say that they wanted more time to complete their work. This was rejected out of hand for the weighty reason that weather over Iraq would be less favourable for an attack later in the year!

It must be noted that having appointed the weapons inspectors and set up the machinery for their work, it is the legal responsibility and prerogative of the same Security Council to decide when to withdraw them. This, Mr Bush is Law, established procedures and propriety, all three. Instead, the respected Secretary-General, Kofi Annan, is told without ceremony that America and Britain are about to attack and unless he, Annan, wants the inspectors to be embroiled in the inevitable air raids he should withdraw them from Iraq. The order to withdraw was illegal and improper, as the Security Council was not consulted. Iraq is therefore justified in accusing the United Nations of betraying their country. The charge is also poignant when it is remembered that the United Nations, through the Security Council got Saddam to destroy some 70 of 100 Al-Samoud missiles ahead of the Anglo-American attack, depriving Iraq of part, and an important part, of its ability to defend itself and confront the aggressors. And we are told this conduct is legal and proper!

The American President is both surprised and upset that some American soldiers are prisoners in Iraqi hands. But he holds that they should not have been presented on television—forgetting that this is the only way the Iraqis can establish facts, in the face of insistence by the partners in crime, that only Iraqis have surrendered. Bush also holds that appearances on television violate the Geneva conventions on prisoners of war. Television became current coin long after the Geneva conventions were signed, Bush needs to reset his calendar!

The Umm Qasr port is used to import food and civil supplies for the Iraqi population, to liberate whom Bush and Blair have sallied forth. No imports have arrived for quite some time and a spokesman for the reputed agency, Oxfam, has said that this is causing untold hardship to ordinary Iraqis and a huge humanitarian disaster is waiting to happen in Basra.

It is time to codify Bush's Law:

1) An unprovoked attack on a sovereign state, which in no way threatens America, is permitted under International Law.
2) To use the United Nations and the Security Council to force Iraq to destroy an important part of its arsenal that could have been used to defend itself is legitimate tactics.
3) To ignore the expressed wishes of the Security Council and the United Nations is both legal and permitted by the UN Charter.
4) Presenting American prisoners on television screens is against the Geneva conventions but Iraqi prisoners are not covered—just like prisoners captured in Afghanistan and held incommunicado at Guantanamo Bay, an American base.

The final idiocy, to use the language of understatement is for Bush to threaten to take Saddam to the International Criminal Court to stand trial for war crimes even as America refuses to sign the convention setting up the Court and does not accept its jurisdiction!

Is that the only reason why Bush cannot be taken to the same Court? Did America have a premonition of what could happen if they accepted the Court's jurisdiction?

Tony Blair by himself is not difficult to handle. The problem is George Bush. Will no one rid us of this meddlesome menace to the rule of law?

26 March 2003

Anglo-American Dilemma

A hornet's nest about their ears

It is said that out of $75 billion for which President Bush requests Congressional authorisation, to cover the cost of his misadventure in Iraq for six months, as much as $67.5 billion is to be for the war and the rest for humanitarian assistance and for rebuilding Iraq. Read this with junior partner Tony Blair's statement to his Parliament on the eve of his visit to Washington, that the UN will certainly be involved in the reconstruction, and the full extent of the hypocrisy is laid bare. First, there is the question of principle. It needs to be stressed that America and Britain defied international opinion and the UN, and launched their attack on Iraq; they are solely responsible for the huge destruction. They now have the gall to assure the UN that they, the UN, will be involved in the reconstruction. The conclusion we are invited to reach is clear—the rest of the world must get together and pay for the damage caused. The effort is likely to cause the two powers some considerable inconvenience. France,

Germany, Russia, China and the rest of the international community against whose expressed wishes the murderous assault was launched after Iraq's ability to defend itself was degraded, may very well refuse to pay. Saudi Arabia, which financed Bush senior's Gulf war, will have difficulties of a different kind this time round. All considered, it seems to be a distinct possibility that America and Britain will have to foot the bill. Also, Iraq ought to have a valid claim in International Law against the two countries for the consequences of international brigandage.

That intentions are less than honest is evident from the measly $7.5 billion, which is left for humanitarian assistance and for Iraq's reconstruction from the total requested of $75 billion. Even out of the $7.5 billion, America has already awarded a contract to its Stevedoring Services of America for $4.8 million to run the port of Umm Qasr. We have not heard that international tenders were invited and the excuse must be that there was no time for scrupulous procedures. It is necessary to warn that if the UN at all agrees to take part in the reconstruction of Iraq, it should do it under its own umbrella and with its own personnel and insist that America and Britain limit their participation to coughing up the lion's share of the cost between themselves. Further, given that the international community will not tolerate Anglo-American occupation of Iraq, any post-Saddam administration should be accountable to the UN only. This will ensure that lucrative oil exploration contracts that Bush and Blair are salivating over will be awarded openly after free and fair bidding under UN auspices and from which American and British companies should, in fairness, be carefully excluded. There must be some accountability for war crimes resulting from the unprovoked and illegal war and will give a new and acceptable meaning to 'Operation Iraqi Freedom'.

The Arab nations have asked for a meeting of the Security Council; no doubt one of the reasons why Blair needs to consult Bush in a hurry. The end of hostilities is the first priority. Not too far behind however, must follow the questions of who is to pay for the damage and who will take charge of the reconstruction. And who will be awarding Oil Exploration Contracts. A point in passing. With this aggression, the sanctions regime and the limited Oil for Food Programme and the no-fly zones are non est. Iraq is free to take its own decisions. This Mr President and Mr Prime Minister is International Law. Unless you admit that whatever the war was about it had nothing to do with 'Iraqi Freedom'.

By the way, whatever happened to Iraq's weapons of mass destruction!

27 March 2003

CAVEAT

Iraq Fights for Survival!

Over a week into the attack on Iraq in the teeth of opposition from the international community in the United Nations, things are going awry. Planning is shown up as based on untenable notions and shallow assumptions. Shias in Basra were expected, as a commentator on BBC put it, to come out with cups of tea to welcome British and American troops devastating their land and killing their people. Instead it is now admitted that Saddam is moving men and armour in and out of Basra to harass the invading hordes from the flanks and from the rear. The illusion that a few tons of aid handed out by the troops would at once get Iraqis to look upon aggressors as liberators was indeed naïve. Aid is now to be handled by the UN. Iraqis are defending their land and it should surprise no one that they are putting up stiff resistance, it is now—officially admitted that it will be a long war. So much armour has been deployed and used with such ferocity that the first lesson of war is forgotten—advance only at the pace dictated by ability to supply the troops. Failure to do this is not due to lack of expertise in the Pentagon; Bush and his companion oilmen want to finish Saddam soon; he is in Baghdad, therefore push headlong there, leaving the flanks and rear for later. The disjointed and often contradictory statements by commanders and politicians, both British and American, before television cameras tell the story.

Those who saw the live press conference on the White House lawns by Bush and Blair could not have failed to notice the tension and the stress on both faces and in body language—they are shocked that Iraq is not alone. Rumsfeld threatens in vain. Bush answers a question on how he will deal with determined opposition from the European Union in particular; given his limitations he avoids it by protesting he has many allies, that he is proud of them and when words run out, he repeats that he is proud of them and will prevail. Blair not so dumb, taking the same question, acknowledges that there are deep differences; that he is worried but hopes it will all come out well in the end.

Major differences have arisen over how to proceed in a post-war Iraq, Blair says again that the UN will have a pivotal role in the reconstruction. Bush will have none of it. The next day in Congressional hearings—a fine American institution—Secretary of State Colin Powell explicitly rules out any role for the UN in decision making in the Baghdad of the future. UN can help with humanitarian aid and he hopes that the UN label will assist governments donate larger sums to the American kitty! Plans visualise retired American diplomats as governors and administrators in Iraq and most important, in charge of awarding oil exploration contracts, which was what the war was about anyway. Clearly rattled, Powell tells Congress what they want to hear—American investment in the war will not be wasted; he will not let anyone else in on the loot. A contract to run Umm Qasr port has gone to an American stevedoring company and the open-ended contract to extinguish oil well fires in Kuwait is awarded to Vice-President Dick Cheney's company. Blair valiantly tries to stress that Iraqi oil is for the Iraqi people but gives the game away by wanting to restart the notorious Oil For Food Programme where half the sales proceeds were used to contain Saddam including paying for weapons inspectors. The world has been fairly warned.

Russia has stiffened its position, France remains adamant, Germany has not shifted one inch, neither has China, nor has the rest of the world. If anything, resentment and opposition to the war is growing, not least in Britain. Let me concede that Bush and Blair both work in a democratic environment, Blair more than Bush who can perhaps wallow in the hysteria a little longer, but not indefinitely.

Two things must be said. Admiration for Iraqi resistance in the face of overwhelming odds is compelling. Everyone would do well to remember that they are not a nation of quislings, illusions to the contrary have been shattered. Next, nothing will change—no Iraqi worth his salt will be seen as an American stooge and prolonged occupation is not on. Secretary-General Kofi Annan laid it out clearly when he set two conditions as paramount, timing it for the Washington summit. One, the sovereignty and integrity of Iraq are not negotiable. Two, the future of Iraq is for the Iraqi people to decide. No wonder Blair told the White House press conference he was planning to see the Secretary-General before he left for home!

Can I ask for the second time—whatever happened to the Iraqi weapons of mass destruction? America has of course, only used weapons of individual destruction!

A word about the regime change, so incessantly canvassed. Saddam may be removed but he will have the last laugh. A regime change in Britain looks a distinct possibility; Bush may last a little longer. But the USA's standing in the world is now for the history books. However, it is still within the power of American public opinion to avoid such a misfortune.

30 March 2003

Chickens Home to Roost

Coalition of the willing is unwilling

Into day eleven of the aggression on Iraq, Bush's coalition of the willing is in deep trouble. In their mad rush, politically dictated, to grab or kill Saddam Hussein in Baghdad, the American army, the best equipped and most mechanised in the world, has got bogged down in the Iraqi desert, without adequate food, water and fuel. It is announced that relief will take six days. The sight of American GIs cleaning their weapons while they wait is not exactly calculated to inspire shock and awe in Saddam Hussein. Suicide attacks against the invaders have commenced. Before Bush complains that this is not in accordance with the Queensbury rules, he should reflect what he has done to bring it about. He has unleashed over a thousand Tomahawk missiles and innumerable precision-guided bombs on a defenceless population. Heavy raids on a daily basis have hit Baghdad to unnerve the population, apart from innumerable Apache helicopter gunships raining death and destruction after the Security Council, under American pressure, used its weapons inspectors to get Iraq to destroy 70 of its Al-Samoud missiles in advance of the attack Bush always intended. Ghengis Khan would have been ashamed. With Bush breaking faith with the UN and the Security Council's betrayal of Iraq, Saddam is entitled to use whatever weapons he has at his disposal. There is a world of difference between using chemical weapons on Kurds to subdue them and facing a choice of using them or be exterminated in a war of aggression for conquest and for oil. Saddam did not start this war; he is fighting for his country and his people.

There are other straws in the wind. Robin Cook who got a standing ovation from all sides in the House of Commons when he resigned over the war on Iraq, has written a stinging article in the British press asking Blair to bring the boys home; it looks as though he is positioning himself to take over when Blair falls on his face. It may be a coincidence but an announcement has been made that as Britain will not be able to sustain a long war, which is likely, the number of British troops in Iraq are to be cut from 45,000 to 5,000. This is not so much an expression of intent as a desperate attempt to calm the opposition in the streets. Bush must be furious. The American headquarters in Qatar have announced that individual soldiers are sending messages to President Bush to assure him that they are praying for him. They should be praying for themselves; at best Bush will leave the White House in disgrace like another Republican President before him for another reason; the poor devils sent to a strange land they do not know and do not understand, are risking their lives for the oilmen in the White House and in Texas.

The same argument goes for suicide attacks, they have started and the Iraqis are saying more will be organised. It must be understood that Iraq has never been a radical Islamic state; Saddam may be a despotic ruler but he has never been a radical Islamist. That he is prepared to confer two medals of honour on the suicide bomber who took four American soldiers with him is a sign of the desperation to which Bush and Bush alone has driven him. The righteous horse Bush may want to mount to show he was right after all is dead under him. Saddam is using this as tactics to unnerve American and British troops and he is succeeding brilliantly. Whether he will be able to go back to his secular credentials is an open question now. All that can be said is that if Iraq too disappears behind the fundamentalist Islamic screen, the responsibility for this will lie squarely with the American President. A message from Osama bin Laden to Saddam Hussein urging him to organise suicide attacks means no more. Before Bush points to it as evidence of terrorism links, he can be assured that it is no such thing. Bush has brought this about by his arrogance, by his ignorance and by his greed.

31 March 2003

CAVEAT

Saddam's Lucky Number!

Thirteen days into the illegal and arrogant aggression on Iraq, the coalition of the willing is not so willing. Adversity is pulling the ragtag coalition apart. Within the Bush administration there are now very visible divisions with Bush and Dick Cheney, the two oilmen on one side, Donald Rumsfeld—who thought he knew better than the Pentagon and choked on his own propaganda that all Iraq except only the Republican Guards and Saddam Hussein were dying to welcome the invading hordes—with Colin Powell dangling somewhere in the middle. Powell and constant ally, Tony Blair seem to be in the same doghouse, for having led Bush into the quagmire that the United Nations proved to be for the wild Texans. Powell is now directed to bully, cajole, or buy out the Turks in the course of a brief visit to Istanbul. He is likely to be disappointed. Fissures are papered over with even more vicious bombing of Iraq and in particular, Baghdad. No dissenting voice is to be tolerated; Peter Arnett, the celebrated commentator who covered the war of papa Bush was sacked unceremoniously by a private television channel for giving it as his opinion on Iraqi television that the American army had got it wrong. All honour to Britain's *Sunday Mirror* for employing him at once. Bush is still seen on television but briefly and without the swagger although still with the conviction of the demented that all is well, because he says so.

Twice in two days Colin Powell is asked to perform before an audience of fanatical Americans and Israelis who punctuate every pause in his words with wild applause. If theatre can win wars, Bush and his oilmen have already won. But the reality is different. Baghdad is taking the punishment, no Iraqis are coming forward to help the coalition; even the Iraqi general supposedly captured turns out to be no general at all. The best-equipped army in the world is bogged down in sand and mud and is short of supplies. Iran, Russia, Syria are warned by Powell of the consequences of coming to Iraq's help. Russia reacts indignantly, Iran keeps its counsel but Syria at the level of its foreign minister, retorts that this war is illegal and Syria has every right to help Iraq to survive. As the going gets tougher for the coalition, American spokesmen will continue to strike out in all directions, a sure sign of an attack of nerves. We are likely to see this nonsense continue for some time longer, until the penny drops that this war cannot be won.

Trying to befriend the Iraqis to persuade them to get rid of Saddam Hussein is no longer policy; shoot anyone approaching American troops is the new order of the day. The reaction is instant and wrong as a bevy of innocent Iraqi women discovered to their cost. Thousands of suicide bombers are reportedly heading for Iraq; a mixed blessing for Saddam who is no Islamic fundamentalist and will have trouble sidelining them after the war is over. For the rest of the world this is a worrisome development.

Suicide bombers are regarded as terrorists; but if they make the difference between the survival of Iraq and allowing the Americans to do what they will with it, a new twist is likely to be given for which the world will pay a heavy price, none so heavy as the United States. And it will be Bush alone who is responsible for the unwelcome development. In passing, the Americans, even at the level of Colin Powell, are still talking of ridding Iraq of its weapons of mass destruction. The evidence they are parading is some anti-chemical suits and headgear found in a warehouse. All things considered, the world must brace itself for some such weapons to be planted and then blamed on the Iraqis. This Mr President is called fabricating evidence in both domestic and International Law.

2 April 2003

Hand it to Bush!

One must hand it to George W Bush Jr. All by his little self, he proves that the ancient maxim— might is right—is alive and well. It seems that the civilising influence of liberal thought, ideals of the French Revolution—*Liberté, Egalité, Fraternité*—fleshing out of Roman Law and jurisprudence over centuries by England with significant contributions from the United States itself, are all being wiped clean from American consciousness. And the decision to change America beyond recognition, to turn its back on international law and civilised intercourse between nations is made by a President, without a popular mandate, in office by a thoroughly questionable interpretation of the American Constitution by the Supreme Court and in gross violation of its spirit.

Every pretence for the cowardly and illegal attack on a sovereign state, advanced with the belief of the bigoted, is blown sky-high. Iraq was to be disarmed and its stock of weapons of mass destruction destroyed. More than two weeks into the war, there is no trace of these weapons but it is confidently stated that they exist leading me to warn of the possibility of their being planted and blamed on the Iraqis. Exposing Americans as victims of their own propaganda and incurring the derision of the world is to be avoided at all costs! Another premise was that Iraqis were dying to be liberated and American and British forces had only to enter the country and people would come out bearing cups of tea in welcome. There were no cups and no tea, only determined resistance. How dare the Iraqis disappoint! The response was unprecedented and relentless, bombardment with Tomahawk cruise missiles, precision-guided bombs, cluster bombs and other lethal weapons, which are nothing if not weapons of mass destruction. Hospitals and schools have been hit; the propaganda is that Iraq is using these to hide guns and ammunition! Is American technology able to peer from on high under hospital beds and school furniture and spot the equipment and is it suggested that it should have been presented for prior approval to the Anglo-American command headquarters?

Americans used to take pride in their commitment to free speech and tolerance of dissenting opinions. As Chairman of the International Press Institute I have had to plead with American colleagues that their view was simplistic and wrong—'If you do not have the equivalent of the First Amendment, there can be no press freedom and no respect for opinions other than one's own.' Peter Arnett, the celebrated reporter, was summarily sacked by NBC under pressure from the Pentagon on Bush's orders. It reminds me of Indira Gandhi's demand to sack Mulgaokar as editor of the *Indian Express* for ignoring her wishes. He stayed thanks to Ramnath Goenka's determined resistance, which I helped to shape. Bush is worse than Indira. The point to note is that Blair could not have prevented the *Daily Mirror* from employing Arnett and to thumb their nose at Bush. I acknowledge that Britain's commitment to free speech and respect for dissent is deeper than the paper on which the First Amendment is printed. This is also the place to disclose that we could have had a correspondent embedded with American troops if we wished; another paper was chosen since *The Statesman*'s independence was too much for the self-appointed champions of liberty—and they were right! It is merely amusing to see the newspaper claim in a self-advertisement that dispatches from their correspondent from the safety of Kuwait are preferable to reports and analysis carried by this newspaper. Have I made my point?

Let me now focus on 'Operation Iraqi Freedom' launched by Bush and Blair. The first to expound on it was Blair outside Downing Street. He called for the resumption of the Food for Oil Programme and chose to forget that it allowed half the proceeds of oil sales to pay for weapons inspectors who ordered the destruction of 70 of Saddam's 100 Al-Samoud missiles. If he had them now he could have deployed them against relentless bombing by Stealth, B-52s, Tomahawk cruise missiles and other agents of 'individual' destruction, as Americans would have it. Bush is familiar with the rake's progress. From destroying Iraq's prohibited weapons, to regime change, to liberating the Iraqi people, he shows he is an accomplished liar. Hitler was more honest. He did not say that the Battle of Britain was fought to liberate the British! 'Operation Iraqi Freedom', indeed!

Blair's assurance that Iraqi oil is for Iraq is answered by Bush refusing any role for the UN except in humanitarian aid and awarding an open-ended contract to put out fires in oil wells to Vice-President Dick Cheney's company. Even Pramod Mahajan would balk at providing such a brazen example of corruption and nepotism. Our

Parliament would erupt in uproar. Does Congress of the United States approve such behaviour? How far will America slip from standards? And how long before it goes through the floor? Donald Rumsfeld said three days ago that after the war, the army would leave and Iraq would be returned to the Iraqi people. He forgot to add—'minus its oil wealth!'

If this is Freedom and Democracy, give me Saddam Hussein every time!

6 April 2003

Exploding Myths and More

New vistas

The bringing of liberation to Iraq in a pyrotechnic display of bombs and missiles has not only devastated the landscape of Baghdad; it has also collapsed the intricate architecture of Western ideology, which has enthralled the world for the past half century.

In a few nights of explosions, fireworks and flames, the carefully wrought theories of development, freedom and affluence with which the West has beguiled the people of the planet have been reduced to ruin. It may prove that the greatest victims of 'friendly fire' are not unfortunate coalition soldiers in the wrong place at the wrong time, but the sacred principles which are the Western gift to the world, and which, until now, have (at least since the war in Vietnam) promised peace and prosperity for all.

The violence against Iraq destroys more than the traces of ancient civilisations. It threatens to bring down the edifice of emancipation which was painstakingly put together after the formal dissolution of the earlier colonial empires.

One of the greatest strengths of the Western ideology has always been its declaration that no such thing exists. Through the years when Communist dogma demanded its tribute of human flesh, the power of the West lay precisely in its claim to have abjured ideology in favour of what works. 'We', the story went, 'are adaptable, pragmatic and undogmatic; we celebrate pluralism and diversity. We have no wish to impose upon people the revelations of scripture, either religious or secular.' This now appears as mendacious as the ideological ornamentation which for so long adorned the fictions of socialism.

First of all, to erase all traces of its colonial maraudings through the world, the West had to subordinate military conquest to politer forms of control. This is where its iconography of wealth has been so potent. The West employed myth and magic to promote itself globally in such a way that it convinced the world that the West is indeed a terrestrial paradise, a compendium of all the dream-places of humanity, the Shangri-La, the Atlantis, the El Dorado, Elysium, the pays *de cocagne,* the land of milk and honey, the site of primal innocence, from which many cultures believe they were expelled, and which can indeed be regained. The West has been a prodigious generator of legend, the begetter of an imagery of easeful indolence, which has entranced an impoverished, suffering world. It has been so successful that people, languishing under the promise that one day this vision will spread to the whole globe, have been unable to curb their desires, and have forsaken their homeplace and set out upon epic journeys and migrations for the fabled shores of peace and plenty. In the process, many have perished; their bodies washed up on foreign beaches, found suffocated in sealed containers or frozen to death in the hold of aircraft. Others, who have reached the destinations of hope, have often found that the fruits of its orchards are inedible, and savour of racism and discrimination.

But this non-ideology, 'embedded' as it has been, within its own visions of luxury, has been the most successful quasi-religious cult in history. It has made converts everywhere. Few have been able to resist its seductive teachings, which tell, not of monsters to be slain and obstacles to overcome, but of an easy passage into the garden of earthly delights. People have abandoned kin and belonging, have betrayed cultures and faiths to find a way into its sites of healing and transcendence.

The Western ideology has been, not a theory, but has been made manifest in an iconography of desire. This is ideology as experience: you can taste and feel it. How thin and threadbare it made all the socialist promises of equality and equal shares of next-to-nothing! How hollow it made promises of an afterlife, the reward of virtue hereafter: the pie-in-the-sky descended, ample and succulent, to be enjoyed in the here-and-now!

This is only one aspect of the wealth-creating miracle. It is calculated to satisfy the pilgrim and the outcast, the wondering multitude.

The second form in which it has been promoted is in a quite separate realm of experience, and its appeal is to the less credulous, the educated and enlightened, those sceptical of the miraculous.

Side by side with the visionary promises, the Western way of wealth has been presented as a severely practical process, a consequence of precise and rigorously formulated steps, which, if taken in proper order and sequence, will lead all the countries of the world to the gates of the earthly paradise.

This is a vision to appeal to technocrats and administrators, to politicians and bureaucracies. What could be more down-to-earth than the suited men arriving in the capital of this or that Third World country in their sharp suits, with their rimless glasses and concentrated stare, sitting in the sequestered boardrooms of privilege, outlining their blueprints, their structural adjustment programmes, their projects of liberalisation, of privatisation, of opening up the dark lands of poverty to the light and freedom of capital, which dispels the shadows of ancient superstition and the dead hand of socialism alike. The path indicated is clear and much travelled, for after all, is it not the one we pursued in our long and arduous journey towards the riches we now wish to place within your reach? Who can resist the sobriety and seriousness of plans for double-digit growth, investment in infrastructure and construction projects, for defence and armaments, for palaces of production and an accelerated facility for exporting the natural advantages of their country! Within a matter of days, the signatures are dry on the documents, the advisers, experts and professionals have moved in, and the secrets of wealth-creation have been whispered in the ear of the elite; and after a celebrated banquet in the Sheraton, the delegation can move on to the next capital city with its identical blueprint for perpetual prosperity.

What a happy marriage it was, of myth and magic blended with science, and presented under the banner of a globalisation that was as benign as it was inevitable. It was a force of nature, irresistible, irreversible.

It was a beautiful and convincing construct. This was the real winner of hearts and minds. What a pity to have wrecked it in a few days by weapons of mass destruction.

The ideology of Western universalism lies shattered like Saddam's palaces. Iraq has demonstrated the nature of the liberation which the peoples of the world must prepare for: they are going to be liberated, not merely—or even primarily—from tyranny and poverty, but from their own sense of identity. This war has made material, in a quite different way from the shining imagery of emancipation, the destruction which this project also inflicts upon all other ancient cultures and civilisations, all other ways of life, all other faiths and belief-systems. They will be dismantled, laid waste, as Iraq has been laid waste, so that on the empty barren emplacements, like the effaced cities of Ur and Babylon, new structures may arise in the image of the invaders. The daisy cutters and bunker busters, the bombs and missiles are precursors of a bogus humanitarianism, behind which the profitable reconstruction contracts are given out, the lucrative oil contracts distributed. And the psyche and sensibility of the people of other religions and ways of life will be transformed, re-shaped to fit the products and fantasies of the transnationals, re-formed to receive the symbols of transcendence. And this will be called freedom.

Western dominance becomes domination and domination becomes global dominion. There was little enough resistance to this version of progress, as long as it maintained a decorous guise of benevolence. In Iraq, military force has replaced economic forces, which, until now, had proved adequate for the purpose of demolishing cultures and rebuilding them with promises of liberation. It would have been better had the war not played out, in a more intense and brutal form, the drama of 'development', whose violence was mitigated by a mixture of magical imagery and bureaucratic assiduity. The effects of the war on the consciousness of the people of the world will not be reversed by the building of shopping malls, highways and vice-regal American buildings. As the pilots fly their interminable bombing sorties over the Ziggurat of Ur and the ruins of Babylon, they can scarcely be expected to give a thought to the mutability of civilisations; even though the spectacle of exultant destruction may presage the dissolution of the brief supremacy of their own.

Jeremy Seabrook
6 April 2003

The author lives in Britain. He has written plays for the stage, TV and radio, made TV documentaries, published more than 30 books and contributed to leading journals around the world.

New Fundamentalism

Equal and opposite of Islamic fundamentalism

Into day 19 of the cowardly attack on Iraq, the Americans and British are not master of a single city in Iraq. They 'almost' control Basra, say the British; they are in the centre of the capital, echo the Americans, adding in the same breath that they will not stay in Baghdad. Having virtually razed Baghdad to the ground in vicious and unremitting air raids, killing and injuring thousands of civilians, it is still a surprise to Americans that Iraqis are not welcoming them as liberators. On the contrary television screens show Saddam Hussein mixing freely with his people in the streets, calm, cool and collected and urging them to fight on and promising them victory. If Saddam appears as a heroic figure with his people cheering him in their hour of trial, Bush's contribution to the creation of the image must be acknowledged.

Bush, described as a born again Christian, betrayed his determination to wage war on Iraq, when he made that extraordinary speech in the Security Council in September 2002 abusing the country and its leader, Saddam Hussein. That there was crass avarice beneath the veneer of religious fanaticism—it seemed like he was leading the Crusades in some speeches—the real motivation was to get his grubby hands on Iraqi oil. Muslim nations without oil reserves or gold deposits or mineral wealth are not in danger. The celebrated winner of the Nobel Prize, Günter Grass, surely had this in mind when he equated Bush and Osama bin Laden as having 'taken God hostage to support their horrible aims'. And he conveys the blinding truth with an economy of words, which is commendable.

Bush is oblivious of the fact that when he faces carefully selected audiences before television cameras to ensure wild applause at every pause in his words, his feet are firmly planted on shifting sands. He begins with the objective of getting rid of Iraq's weapons of mass destruction; when weapons inspectors fail to find any, he gets Colin Powell to present fabricated evidence from some old web sites. When the subterfuge is exposed, he tries to get another resolution from the Security Council authorising war. Against determined opposition from France, Germany, Russia and even China, he retreats saying the earlier resolution 1441 authorises war anyway, inviting the obvious retort that if he thought it was enough why did he try so hard to get another resolution? Somewhere along the line is added the objective of getting rid of Saddam Hussein, because 'That man tried to kill my Dad in 1993'. 'Regime change' was the inelegant phrase used. By that time he had massed the most extensive weaponry of mass destruction in history—Tomahawk cruise missiles, precision guided bombs, and the vicious cluster bombs, designed to explode on touch over a huge

New Fundamentalism

area to ensure maximum civilian casualties, Bush codenames the international banditry—'Operation Iraqi Freedom!' We have a taste of the Freedom reserved for Iraqis. Umm Qsar port would be operated by an American stevedoring company and an open-ended contract for putting out oil fires is given to Vice-President Dick Cheney's company. Only a spurious religious fervour can sustain such corruption and nepotism. Bush allows the UN only a role in humanitarian aid, which would not have been necessary if he, Bush, had not wrought such destruction in the first place. It is made clear even to ally Tony Blair that America expects to recoup itself for the billions spent on the war from sales of Iraqi oil.

Oxford English Dictionary did not know what they were letting themselves in for when they accepted the word 'Bushism'. Now there must be another entry—'Bushy Fundamentalism'—the equal and opposite of Islamic fundamentalism. Saddam is a despot but he is no Islamist; if he is now speaking of *jihad*, it is Bush who has driven him to it.

8 April 2003

CAVEAT

Thumping the Table!

All we have had so far and the war is into the fourth week, are some chemical suits and empty drums. As a piece of sophistry, the article published in a New Delhi newspaper on 8 April 2003 by Robert D Blackwill, the distinguished Ambassador in India for the United States of America, has seldom been equalled and never surpassed. "Make no mistake," thunders the Ambassador: "This war has a firm basis in International Law!" We do not need assertions; we need legally sustainable arguments. Are we told that there is approval of the Security Council for the attack on Iraq with thousands of Tomahawk missiles, precision bombs and the special weapon of mass destruction—the cluster bomb—which has caused horrendous civilian casualties? We have not one but three Security Council Resolutions offered as justification—numbered 678, 687 and 1441. Resolution 678 of 29 November 1990—not January 1991 as stated—is in the Ambassador's words, authority "to drive Iraq from Kuwait and to restore peace and security in the region". Having achieved that objective in the Gulf war, the resolution can have no further effect and cannot be resurrected to deal with a new situation. Or is His Excellency under the impression that driving Iraq from Kuwait is the same as driving into Iraq from Kuwait as his boss did on 19 March 2003? The polite response to the assertion that 678 plainly authorises war twelve years later, must be that there is nothing plain about it!

Resolution 687 has no application as it deals with the post-Gulf war situation and can, in no sense, be read to authorise war a decade later. Resolution 1441 was indeed a warning to Iraq to comply and resulted in the return of the Inspectors to Iraq. I call to witness that Iraq did accept the inspectors; that they did return and that in reports to the Council they did express satisfaction with their work and asked for time to complete it. Only the United States and Britain refused and instead demanded that Iraq immediately prove a negative—they do not hold any prohibited weapons—a fallacy in logic, although I do not expect either the Ambassador or his boss to understand, let alone accept it. Suffice it to say that great confidence was expressed that now that the invaders were all over the country they would find the weapons in question. All we have had so far and the war is into the fourth week, are some chemical suits and empty drums, which 'could' have held substances, which 'might' have had some gases or chemicals as ingredients.

The Ambassador anticipates the question—if 1441 was considered adequate to go to war why did America and Britain strive so manfully against the majority of the international community to get a resolution expressly authorising war? The Ambassador's answer is short, simple and wrong. 'It was to go that extra step'. This is merely asinine. Not once during the long hours of debate, replete with threats against all who dissented, did either the USA or the UK make it plain that they relied on 1441 and were asking for the new resolution because they liked going for a walk! Afterthoughts are not arguments, Mr Ambassador! A month ago President Bush said he had the support of 30 unnamed countries and this was disputed. In your article you say the number is nearly 50. Who is in charge of the head count, Mr Blackwill?

Iraq is accused of continually changing its story. President Bush is a past master at doing just that. He started with a diatribe against Iraq and Saddam Hussein and declared that his objective was limited to ridding Iraq of weapons of mass destruction. When a series of reports of weapons inspectors did not fit the premeditated intent to grab Iraqi oil, a new twist was added—'this guy tried to kill my Dad in 1991'. Saddam was asked to go into exile, which the Ambassador will accept does not feature in any of the Resolutions he relies upon. Where is UN authority for the demand for 'regime change'? By the time Bush launched the attack his objective had been elevated to restoring Freedom to the Iraqis! Did Iraq ever beg the Security Council for freedom, like freedom to award a contract to run an Iraqi port to an American agency and freedom to grant a lucrative oil contract to American Vice-President Dick Cheney's company? What is the level of the reasoning, Mr Blackwill?

Table thumping by Ambassador Blackwill and his boss in Washington, insisting that their actions are legal is not a substitute for reason and argument and fails to impress. A wise professor at my Law College once counselled us—If you are weak on the facts and strong on the law, stress the law. If you are weak on the law and strong on the facts stress the facts. If you are weak both on the facts and the law, thump the table! There is altogether too much thumping around here, Mr Ambassador! And it is not intimidating anybody, least of all the Iraqis, despite the sponsored television images!

10 April 2003

And now Journalists!

America and Britain must answer

There is now irrefutable evidence that American troops trained the guns of their tanks on the Palestine Hotel in Baghdad, knowing fully well that foreign journalists covering the war were billeted there. We have the head of Al Jazeera TV taking a press conference in Qatar to say that before the start of hostilities they had given the exact location of their headquarters in Baghdad to the Americans so that accidents could be avoided. Their office, elsewhere in the city was deliberately destroyed. The attack on Abu Dhabi TV makes it three targets in a row in one day! The Russian Ambassador gave the Americans details of the route he would take to get out of Baghdad and his convoy was attacked. The first reaction of the invaders, supposedly trying to elevate Iraqi standards, was to brazenly lie and seek to blame it on Iraqi fire. They were forced to back down but still justify their act by saying that Baghdad is a 'combat zone' and safety cannot be guaranteed. Eye-witness accounts of BBC correspondents and other professionals clearly establish that there was no fire emanating from the Palestine Hotel. To target the hotel was deliberate and in breach of Protocol 1 of the Geneva Convention's Article 52(1).

The respected human rights organisation, Amnesty International says in a press release, that the Palestine Hotel was a civilian object protected under international humanitarian law that should not have been attacked. If it had demonstrably been used for military purposes it should not have been attacked by a tank shell clearly incapable of careful targeting in this case.

Tony Blair jumps into the fray with a message of his own to the Iraqi people dated 6 April. He promises that after the war, Iraq will be run by and for the Iraqi people. "Not by America, not by Britain, not by the UN—though all of us will help—but by you the people of Iraq." It is already announced that a former US General, Jay Garner, by name will head the post-war authority and Blair is busy naming a second in command who will be a British national. A quisling is however being groomed to take over once it is clear that he will agree to whatever is required of him. He is an Iraqi, Ahmad Chalabi, one of those in exile who give cover to US objectives. To make things crystal clear, he is a favourite of the Pentagon. A war for turf is already under way in Washington between Colin Powell's Department of State and Donald Rumsfeld's Defence Department as to who will call the shots. President Bush will presumably decide and there are no prizes for guessing which way he will jump.

Blair also promises that the money from Iraqi oil will be 'yours'. Under current rules of construction which one hopes still apply, he promises the money to the Iraqi people. In view of the positions taken in Washington, at the most the money will be what is left over after America has helped itself, witness Colin Powell's unambiguous pointer to the billions America has spent on the war and for which it clearly expects to be reimbursed.

In the circumstances Tony Blair could have spared himself embarrassment by refraining from issuing any message and if he had to, by not ending with the words—"In the spirit of true friendship and goodwill, we will do our utmost! ..." Does he think the elusive cups of tea in welcome will now appear!

10 April 2003

CAVEAT

Calling the Price!

It is not always that the human spirit triumphs over brute force and murderous intent, especially when backed by a cynical disregard of International Law and buttressed by the most formidable array of weapons of mass destruction ever assembled. Iraq had been weakened by twelve years of inhuman sanctions, approved by the Security Council, later treated with conspicuous disdain by the United States and another country with an hitherto proud record of standing up for itself. As soon as the UN showed signs that it had a mind of its own and was not prepared to be bullied by its biggest defaulter, the attitude changed. To hear Bush and Blair tell Iraqis how disinterested is their concern for their freedom and welfare and how these two outlaws propose to bring prosperity to Iraq, with womenfolk liberated, children going to the best schools, medical care not seen anywhere yet, food and jobs going a-begging and in sum enjoying a standard of living such as they have not achieved themselves, is to gape in awe at their temerity in spewing promises so much at variance with their brutality, their vulgarity and their greed. Two images impress. As the respected former editor of *The Times*, Simon Jenkins, says in this newspaper, it recalls the pretensions of the East India Company, which came to India to trade and stayed to rule. But also, to realise how amateurish, by comparison was Goebbels, propaganda minister of Hitler's Third Reich, credited with the discovery that a lie repeated often enough takes on the mantle of truth!

Reactions in Washington and London are muted but not due to any proper sense of modesty or a sudden attack of conscience; the penny has just dropped. They realise that in international law, they need the UN, if only as a fig leaf to lift sanctions, not to help the Iraqi people but to help themselves to Iraqi oil. The Food for Oil Programme must be amended before they can reimburse themselves for the cost of the war and only the Security Council can do so. That is why even Bush is now saying that the UN will have a pivotal role and when asked to explain the contradiction with his earlier assertion of the rights of the victor, he only repeats that when he says a 'pivotal role', he means a pivotal role! The man must be under compelling advice not to stray from his text because any exhibition of his chronic foot-in-mouth disease can upset the whole applecart. For good measure, Colin Powell again restricts the UN to humanitarian aid.

Apart from the illegality of it all, the American General Jay Garner, viceroy of Iraq in waiting, will be saddled with an Iraqi émigré tutored in the USA, with a thoroughly questionable past, to be the Iraqi face of an interim administration. His principal backer is Donald Rumsfeld; even General Garner does not want Chalabi. I was astonished to hear one of those instant American experts paraded on television, give it as his considered view that the question is not about his reputation but whether he can establish himself as leader of the new administration in Baghdad! Obviously, what is sauce for the goose is pure nectar for the gander!

The real war in Iraq is only just beginning; with the central authority in ruins, law and order, maintenance of essential supplies, a police force and all the wherewithal of an administration likely to fall well short of the capabilities of the occupying powers as Shias, Kurds, Sunnis and various tribal factions fight it out to fill the power vacuum even as they resist the occupying troops. Iraq is becoming ungovernable. The task will also be hit by the notoriously limited American attention span. That is why America is now discovering such virtues in the UN it has ignored so contemptuously.

The first task of the occupying powers will be to restore order; the cheers of coalition troops as they topple statues of Saddam Hussein will die in the distance as they run out of statues. Bells will stop ringing and the drums they have been beating will cease to sound. Then what? The only organised political entity that Saddam allowed, the Ba'ath party, is destroyed but remnants remain to harass the occupying forces indefinitely. It will be a grave mistake for the UN to take comfort that at last their role is recognised. There is no such admission, only attempts, with cold calculation to shift responsibility and costs elsewhere. Secretary-General Kofi Annan should work with Europe and the rest of the world to stand aside and let America and Britain repair the damage they have so wantonly caused—economically first, but also politically and socially. When they throw up their hands in despair, will it be the time for Annan to call his price. But not till then!

And before they soil their hands the UN must require America and Britain to produce those weapons of mass destruction, not the ones they have used in Iraq, but the ones Iraq was supposed to hide.

13 April 2003

Our Way of Life

New vistas

In his solemn address to the nation on the outbreak of war, Tony Blair spoke of the dangerous mixture of terrorists and rogue states, the ostensible 'cause' of the pre-emptive combat. He said: "They hate our freedom, democracy and way of life."

Blair has used this phrase more than once recently. He is clearly signalling something to the British people. But what, exactly? What do these few innocent words mean?

He is directly echoing George W Bush, who referred to 'those who hate all civilisation and culture and progress'. 'Our way of life' has an agreeably inclusive ring: but who are the 'we' in this comprehensive term? The total self-identification of Blair with Bush suggests that Britain and the USA share an inseparable common destiny; a suggestion that in an undeclared and bloodless War of Dependence, Britain chose its transformation into an outpost of the American imperium. This, no doubt, is why 'our way of life' embraces such hallowed traditions as the have-a-nice-day culture, serial killings, obesity and commerciogenic malnutrition, gun-crime, mind-altering substances for minds which have already been changed too often, the vast industries devoted to escapism in the most wealthy—and escapist—societies the world has ever known. Are these spectral companions of our advantage, or just regrettable by-products, like garbage, toxins and the environmental ruin which it also produces?

The maintenance of 'our way of life' encodes something more than these pleasant adornments of privilege. It means exactly what it did when first enunciated by George Bush Senior before the Rio Summit in 1992, in his admonition that "The American way of life is not up for negotiation."

This simple expression is no vague pietism. It stands for, and symbolises, something very precise and material indeed; and that is the preservation of privilege. Everybody knows this. It is part of the semaphores and signals whereby the rich affirm to one another their determination to keep what they have. All rhetoric about poverty-abatement, halving the numbers in poverty, closing the gap between rich and poor is purely decorative, and remains subordinate to it.

This way of life depends crucially upon institutionalised and growing global inequality. This is no political fiction: the income gap between the richest fifth of the world's people and its poorest fifth, measured by per capita income increased from 30:1 in 1960 to 74:1 in 1997.

Since the end of socialism, the flow of wealth from poor to rich has been sustained principally by economic instruments. The management of growing social injustice has been entrusted to the organisations which have so spectacularly uplifted the poor of earth—the IMF, WB, WTO and bilateral arrangements between rich and poor countries. It seems that this orderly one-way flow of resources is now in danger. The peaceable transfer of resources, wealth and treasure from the poorest parts of the world to their rightful owners is called into question by terrorism. Sterner measures are called for. And what could be more stern than war?

It is widely acknowledged by our leaders, in their less belligerent moments, that injustice, the growing despair of the poor are, at least in part, central to the creation of terrorists. They sometimes concede that only by addressing the gross inequalities thrown up by globalisation shall we destroy the environment in which the malignancy flourishes.

So how is this compatible with their admission that going to 'war' will lead to a heightened risk of attack? If all the alerts and warnings, and exhortations to vigilance were not bogus and purely for effect; if they surrounded Heathrow with tanks on the holy festival of Id, this must be because they know their actions are likely to generate violent reactions. If Blair explicitly stated the invasion of Iraq is likely to increase the likelihood of terror in Britain and elsewhere, then clearly the war has purposes other than the extirpation of terror.

The idea that Iraqi oil is going to be put in a UN trust for the people of Iraq, Rumsfeld's indignant declaration that the oil is the property of the Iraqi people, are as plausible as the commitment to an orderly reshaping of the whole world in the image of the West. The West needs the resources of the world to pursue its own core necessity of constant growth and expansion. And we will fetch these resources from wherever they may be, no matter which nation, country or other inconvenient geographical entity chances to sit astride them: the forests of Cambodia and Brazil, the diamonds of Angola, the fish of the Lakshadweep, the coffee of Guatemala and Tanzania, adventitiously lodged in these territories, belong in the global market; and our way of life demands that is where they will go.

To prevent any disruption of this process, nothing is unthinkable, not even war, regime change or even the increased threat of terrorism. We must be prepared for more of what we have already seen, since we are primary causal agents of its existence.

This is the subtext of Tony Blair's sombre warning to the British people.

Our way of life is threatened, above everything, by a more just economic order. It is not so much that economic injustice creates hatred and resentment—although it assuredly does—as that injustice is built into the very structures and institutions that protect, enhance and further our way of life; and nothing is going to be done to change that. In other words, the intensification of inequalities that have led to the three richest individuals in the world—Bill Gates, the Sultan of Brunei and the Walton family—commanding more wealth than the annual income of 600 million people living in the world's poorest countries, is not going to be jeopardised, least of all by the beneficiaries of global privilege, even when these operate under the flag of convenience of 'poverty-abatement'.

This is why we face the prospect of endless war. War on terror metamorphoses into war on the poor. So if the one-sided attack on Iraq, with its foregone conclusion, was not—as a majority of the world's people believe—about terror, neither was it gratuitous.

When Tony Blair says they hate 'our way of life', this is what he is telling us: the way of life, which prioritises the most trivial whim of wealth over the necessities for survival of the poor, is going to create more rage and more violence. We must adjust to that unpleasing connection, and meet the 'threat' with all necessary means. But you can't just go and attack the poorest people on earth without good reason. They have to harbour terror. Afghanistan, Iraq—two down. How many to go?

We live in a double consciousness: perpetual peril on the one hand, and business as usual on the other. Just as 'shock and awe' and the fireballs over Baghdad throw a surreal light over the democracy and humanitarianism in the name of which this barbarism is conducted, so the noble phrases that call us to the patriotic duty of stoicism and determination eerily illuminate the way of life, which, Blair tells us, others hate so much. It suggests that its very normality is a major contributory factor to the disturbance, upheaval and growing injustice of the world. And who is going to declare war on that?

Jeremy Seabrook
13 April 2003

CAVEAT

Catastrophic Success!

Both George Bush and Tony Blair continue to bleat about Iraq's weapons of mass destruction, although none have been found and their forces are all over Iraq. This makes the world nervous because both have shown intolerance of any view but their own on anything connected even remotely with Saddam Hussein. The list of those wanting to know the location of these elusive weapons increases by the hour—the latest to join the chorus is President Putin who openly allows himself to think that they exist in order to bring the maximum pressure on America and Britain to produce them. The comment of the US Commander, General Tommy Franks, that it remains the second objective but 'may take months or years' to achieve, increases uneasiness around the world. Secretary of State Colin Powell was shown to have used questionable material to argue his case in the Security Council. And I have warned explicitly in these columns, that something may be planted on purpose to have it 'discovered' later As Americans would say there is clear and present danger of some such manoeuvre being tried to get out of an acute embarrassment.

A great deal was made of an Iraqi general who surrendered to the Americans, helping to find these elusive weapons; the hype evaporated when he said on television that he had told the weapons inspectors there were no such weapons and he was telling the truth. The Bush brigade does not give up easily. Americans have said they have a long list of Iraqis who disturb their peace and whom they want to reach. Hope springs eternal that some Iraqi somewhere will be ready to cooperate and find it to his advantage to do so. Americans have not named their price for the cooperation they seek but their hopes remain high. Faith in the almighty dollar is unshaken although promises of vast sums for any lead to Osama bin Laden have not been taken up. And there is general agreement that Osama is alive and well; even General Musharraf says so. He should know; he brought Osama and Mullah Omar out of Afghanistan in safe air corridors granted by a grateful Bush. American intelligence has told the President but he takes no notice because it interferes with his design not to blame Pakistan for anything. Would Congress care to examine the heads of the various American intelligence agencies in their very effective Congressional hearings? They may learn something that may surprise them. But Bush may no longer be interested in Osama; he has a new hate figure in Saddam Hussein!

The American penchant for pithy formulations is having a free run. We have had WMD or weapons of mass destruction. We are only allowed to know what they are not. They are not the newly developed mother of all bombs, the 2,000 pounder that makes huge craters and spreads death and destruction, They are not the cluster bombs specifically designed to cause maximum civilian casualties. Saddam is accused of having used poison gas against the Kurds years ago; this is trotted out as justification for war in the present. However, they do not accept, on a parity of reasoning, that the United States being the only country in the world to have unleashed atomic bombs on defenseless civilians, not once but twice in Hiroshima and Nagasaki needs to be watched. Are atomic bombs benign weapons, Mr President? Then we have 'Operation Iraqi Freedom', which is the antithesis of freedom anywhere. Apparently there are seven objectives of the war not listed before the Security Council, let alone approved by it.

There is an expression for every discomfort. When a respected correspondent of the BBC says that the chaos, the anarchy, the looting and the disorder are regarded as worse than Saddam's regime, Tony Blair's spokesman takes no time at all to accuse him of something akin to treason. Rumsfeld thinks he paints a broad picture. It takes some doing to suggest that the chaos and anarchy, not forgetting the stripping and destruction of the historic Baghdad Museum while American troops look on is all a manifestation of the new freedom from the Saddam legacy, gifted by America! He calls it 'Catastrophic Success'! It has a nice self-congratulatory ring about it, hasn't it? He must hope that it will not all degenerate into 'Catastrophe' simpliciter!

Americans are nothing if not fanciful and innovative!

15 April 2003

CAVEAT

Iraq is not a Game!

It must be the height of the silly season in Washington and London. We have the visual of President Bush moving with a swagger that puts one in mind of improbable Western films of earlier times, insisting that Syria possesses chemical weapons, that it must not give asylum to Saddam Hussein, his family or friends and that America would be seriously displeased if it did not obey. Thoroughly alarmed by the mental illness of his close friend, Tony Blair hastens to deny that Syria is the next on his list or on any list for that matter. A few days later Colin Powell tries to smooth ruffled feathers although he can hardly repudiate everything his boss said.

Ahmad Chalabi, the quisling selected by Defence Secretary, Donald Rumsfeld, to run Iraq for him has taken cover; another stooge is attending the conclave of Iraqis convened by General Jay Garner under orders of the Pentagon or the State Department, we cannot tell for sure. A thoroughly discredited émigré, Chalabi is waiting in the wings for the curtain call to take over. It may never come. What America did not expect was a spontaneous gathering of 20,000 Shia Muslims, within hailing distance of Garner's gathering, loudly protesting that they would not accept American tutelage; the gathering already divided, melted in confusion promising to foregather later. Facile American assumptions lie in tatters. Shias are supposed to hate Saddam, it is apparent that they hate Americans more. The welcoming cups of tea never materialised. Will you now please take off that Iraqi flag you are wearing on your lapel, General?

The pillage and plunder of Iraq by the invaders is under way but it is early days yet to tell whether it will all explode in their face. Bush and Blair are saying that Iraqi oil, meant for the Iraqi people, will be used to rebuild Iraq. Translated into American intentions shorn of pretence, it means that the oil will be extracted by companies chosen by America, that it will be sold at prices fixed by America, to countries selected by America. No medieval conqueror could ask for more.

The Security Council remains troubling for America and Britain. In an effort to tame it, Jack Straw, the British Foreign Secretary, makes a most extraordinary statement. He urges the Security Council to "forget past divisions over Iraq and accept the new reality created by the US-led invasion". He has the gall to lecture the world. "It is the responsibility of all Security Council members not to play games but to recognise this reality." I am reliably informed that Jack Straw is a barrister and of some note. Will he please answer some questions?—Who divided the Security Council in the first place? Did or did not weapons inspectors say repeatedly and unequivocally that they found no such weapons and did they not commend Iraq for its cooperation? Was not America exposed as having used thoroughly questionable material

Iraq is not a Game!

in making the case against Iraq? Has not Hans Blix, the Chief Weapons Inspector, resigned and has he not accused America of a premeditated decision to go to war? Were not America and Britain pitted against the majority of the Council and against the vociferous opposition of France, Russia and China—three veto-wielding powers? Did you not issue an ultimatum to Saddam Hussein to go into exile and with arguments—flawed on facts and in law—did you seek, let alone obtain Council approval? Finally, Mr Straw, it is not possible to 'forget' the gross breach of International Law simply because it is inconvenient that it should be remembered.

You and Tony Blair support the American argument that Security Council Resolutions 678, 687 and 1441 authorise war anyway. Will you agree that Resolution 678, authorising force to drive Iraq from Kuwait, lapsed on completion of the task in 1991 and is not available more than a decade later to wage another war? Resolution 687 deals with the post-Gulf war situation and can have no application. As for Resolution 1441, if you thought it authorised war anyway why did you try so desperately to have another resolution for the purpose? I have asked to see the case for opinion you submitted to lawyers who advised you that your war has legal sanction and I am still waiting! We follow British jurisprudence in India and are proud of it; however if this is the level of legal expertise available in Britain today, must I not advise our government to look elsewhere! Are you familiar with the concept of crime and punishment, Mr Straw? Isn't it axiomatic that no criminal should be allowed to profit from his crime? Both Bush and Blair have acted like war criminals under International Law. The least you can do is to offer to rebuild Iraq at your cost even if your arrogance will not permit you to appear in sackcloth and ashes. Instead you accuse the Security Council of playing games! Iraq is not a game, Mr Secretary!

18 April 2003

In the Sands of Time!

In the Caveat—*Calling the Price!*—13 April 2003, I thought President Bush would need the Security Council to lift sanctions so that American companies can extract all the Iraqi oil they want and amend the Food for Oil Programme to remove limits on the volume extracted. Otherwise Bush's plans to recoup the costs of his utterly private war from oil proceeds will flounder. It takes the wild-eyed Rambo only three days to prove me right. On 16 April 2003, Bush pronounces *ex cathedra*, that sanctions be lifted and Food for Oil Programme amended since Saddam is gone and his regime overthrown. Bush lacks any sense of finesse, which, I concede, Tony Blair retains. Blair intones deadpan that time to lift sanctions has not arrived. He wants to ensure that Bush, Cheney and Rumsfeld do not run with all the contracts and British companies can participate in the loot. Blair knows Bush well and the strain is showing.

Russian President Vladimir Putin is an old pro and has seen through the game. He has taken a position, well supported in International Law that as sanctions were imposed to compel discovery of prohibited weapons, any question of lifting them must await proof of existence of the weapons or admission that they do not exist. As US Commander General Tommy Franks says it will take months or years to reach a conclusion, it follows that sanctions cannot be lifted any time soon. Apart from Russian roulette, Russians are great chess players; Putin has moved a pawn and called checkmate!

Bush's cup of woe is full to overflowing. For only the second time, former President Bill Clinton has intervened with exquisite timing. He takes Bush to the cleaners over foreign policy pursued since September 11. Choosing his words carefully, Clinton deplores abuse heaped on France and Germany saying, "it was a gross overreaction to punish those that didn't join the war in Iraq. I think to look around and try to get even with the rest of the world would be an error. We have to bring the world together". Then the punch—"If you can't kill, jail and occupy all your adversaries, sooner or later you have to make a deal." In a rapier thrust President Clinton adds—"We are asking everybody to sacrifice to fight the war on terror. A hundred of our fellow citizens gave their lives in Iraq. That's a big sacrifice. ... We have asked poor people to give up job training funds. We have asked something from just about everybody. But the only sacrifice demanded of the rich was to accept a tax cut!" Clinton is left-handed so I have to say that in a right-handed compliment, he suggests that 'President George Bush's leadership team may have made poor decisions about the Iraq conflict because individuals were under stress. Sometimes when people are under stress, they hate to think—and it's the time when they most need to think.' You have said it all, Mr President and said it brilliantly!

George W Bush is bested by just about everybody. He has mortally offended Syria by his reckless charge that it is hiding chemical weapons. Arabs have lost no time in getting together and handing Bush a stunner. They have called for a nuclear free zone in the entire Middle East and tabled an appropriate resolution in the Security Council. The move is clearly aimed at Israel and Bush finds himself on the horns of a dilemma. He cannot be seen to oppose destruction of nuclear weapons and he can no more ask Israel to disarm than fly. The Jewish lobby on the East Coast will have him for breakfast.

Meanwhile Tony Blair's leadership is in peril. His party is in revolt and the public mood is strongly and increasingly against his policies in Iraq, particularly those, which suggest he is barely able to move out from Bush's shadow. He was ready to resign if he lost the vote for war; he will have to go if he loses the peace. Jack Straw's demand that the Security Council accept the 'reality' of the Anglo-American invasion and 'forget' the rest, including the blatant illegality, is a piece of arrogant nonsense, which would be difficult to emulate. Britain is a proud nation, deservedly so. Churchill's equation with Roosevelt in World War II was an alliance of equals, the old country's experience married to the might of the new. The nation that declared war on Nazi Germany to stand up for Poland cannot take kindly to a prime minister who jumps into Bush's lap by instinct, if only to advance the interests of British oil companies.

President Clinton is an experienced politician with a first class mind. He can be expected to continue what he has begun. He is obviously concerned for the good name of his country. There is no place here for the religious and necessarily bigoted right; Bush should prepare for transformation into an intensely private person come November 2004 and his personal papers may not interest any library. Cowboys may swagger and mouth inanities, they leave no footprints in the sands of time.

20 April 2003

CAVEAT

Cold Feet over Iraq!

In response to the Caveat—*Iraq is not a Game!*—of 18 April, I have a letter from the British High Commission in Delhi, signed by one Gerry McCrudden, First Secretary, Press and Public Affairs. It runs into seven paragraphs over two pages and I have given it close attention. There is no way I can deal with comments like—'I am also very sure that the citizens of Iraq think very differently to the views expressed in your article'. It is presumptuous, to say the least, for representatives of a country which invaded Iraq without cause, inflicted horrendous damage, killed and maimed thousands of civilians and is now asking everyone, including the UN and Security Council, to forget it ever happened, to claim that they are privy to the views of the victims to the exclusion of professional commentators!

The letter makes two points requiring a reply. Debates in the Security Council clearly show that Inspectors were mandated to find the prohibited weapons that Saddam was supposed to have accumulated and threatened the world. We now have the astonishing statement that this was not the business of Inspectors at all! 'They were not detectives', we are told, 'it was not their job to find the WMDs'. No doubt this ludicrous position is taken to hide the fact that no such weapons were found by the Inspectors or by the invading hordes. If it was not for the Inspectors to find them, then please answer two questions. Is it or is it not true that Hans Blix has repeatedly told the Security Council that no weapons of mass destruction were found but has asked for time to complete inspections? Two, did the inspectors not discover and ensure the destruction of as many as 70 Al-Samoud missiles? Blix has accused America and by association the UK, of harbouring a predetermined intention to go to war. And contrary to your assertion, he is willing to go back and complete the task assigned to the inspectors. What are you afraid of? That inspectors will say Iraq was and is, free of weapons of mass destruction?

The other point is the legality of the operation. The letter quotes the British Attorney-General for the view that the operation was legal. A lawyer myself, I respect those in bands and gown. However the give-away is the date of his alleged Opinion. You quote it as 17 March 2003. By that time, Bush and Blair had asked Saddam to go into exile or face war. It follows therefore, that the Attorney-General was approached after the decision was made to go to war. So much for your concern for International Law and pious pronouncements on the subject of the Rule of Law, the UN Charter, and International Humanitarian Law! Besides if the Opinion were against you, do you seriously contend that Bush and Blair would have retraced their steps? Why do you use a respected Counsel so cruelly?

Your concluding sentence lauds the freedoms such as the UK and India take for granted, adding that in your opinion, the Iraqis deserve nothing less. Did they submit for your decision what they deserve? Language is a beautiful medium; I am a great admirer of it myself. But when used to mouth platitudes drained of meaning and in fact designed to cover the greed for Iraqi oil for which contracts are already being distributed by the USA, without reference to, let alone the sanction of the UN, it leaves a nauseating taste behind. You devote the second paragraph, the longest in your letter to quote Tony Blair. Despite the affection and respect I have for him personally, I am constrained to say that until there is a reasonable correlation between the words used by the Prime Minister and the actions of his government, you will pardon me if I treat them as eminently dispensable. In case you think I am avoiding an answer, let me assert that in earlier pieces I have dealt with his words and the hypocrisy they betray and I have no wish to embarrass him further.

Blair has said often that British troops will not stay in Iraq a day longer than necessary. Does the Prime Minister agree with President Bush that it could take as long as two years? Bush adds that he is laying the foundation for democracy in Iraq. Who asked him to do that? Will he next sow seeds of democracy in Pakistan? And thereafter benefit North Korea? No! Neither country has anything comparable to Iraqi oil. In Churchill's immortal phrase in another context, he can expect only—'blood, toil, tears and sweat'. Bush now says Saddam is dead. This is a repeat of motions he went through to avoid the question—where is Osama? On WMDs, Bush echoes my correspondent. Saddam had them. But he says he may have 'destroyed them', moved them, or hid them. If he allows that he destroyed them, wasn't that what he was supposed to do? Or is he to be punished for having had them in some form, at some time, at some place? In which case what about the undeniable fact that America had atomic weapons in 1945 and that it used them, not once but twice against defenceless civilians in Hiroshima and Nagasaki? Arguments on a parity of reasoning are logical.

For the standing of Great Britain, which has a reputation extending over centuries, I beg your government to set a distance from America until that country sheds the Bush legacy and recovers its equilibrium.

29 April 2003

CAVEAT

The Rest of the World!

As President George Bush continues to flounder in his bid to convince Iraqis that he is the Saviour come, leaving ally Tony Blair to contemplate a meeting with his Maker, he seems not to feel the ground slipping under his feet. General Jay Garner, Donald Rumsfeld's choice to run Iraq, started badly. Lecturing bewildered Iraqis on the virtues of getting rid of Saddam, never mind the cost in chaos, confusion, horrendous damage and stifling foreign occupation and with an Iraqi flag pinned to his tunic for effect, Garner was clearly out of his depth. His meeting of Shia invitees, led to a spontaneous response from a 20,000 strong gathering nearby—get out of Iraq! Garner ends the meeting hastily, although he seems to have heeded advice as regards sporting the Iraqi flag; indeed he has not appeared in military uniform again. Iraq's neighbours meeting on Saudi soil ask the US to leave Iraq to the Iraqis and go home. Another meeting of Arab states checkmate Bush demanding a nuclear free zone throughout the Middle East including Israel.

Bush's response is typical. He replaces the hapless Garner with a former State Department official, Paul Bremer, to head the interim Iraqi administration; there is no reason to suppose that cosmetic changes will work. Bush surrounds himself with like-minded grubby advisors and to complicate his life, there is a visible turf war between Defense and State. Siding with one, then the other, the third choice is Condoleezza Rice, his National Security Advisor, more rabid than Rumsfeld, proving that it is possible to jump from the frying pan into the fire. But Bush's focus on oil never wavers. There is now an American oilman from Shell in the Iraqi Oil Ministry to ensure that the purpose of the war is not diluted. Bush has said, America will not leave Iraq any time soon; it will take two years. He needs the time to bring 'democracy' to Iraq, having trampled underfoot International Law and the Geneva conventions in the process.

The elusive weapons of mass destruction are a huge embarrassment for Bush. Periodically it is announced that something suspicious is spotted. Recently it was traces of chemicals in drums that could be used to make 'dirty' nuclear bombs. Risk of falling into terrorist hands was the kite flown. IAEA agency in Vienna promptly demands access to verify as is their duty and their right under international obligations. Taken aback the US promptly retreats; the material is not dangerous after all! To their credit, Americans are not good at deception, *markirovka,* as the Russians would say. Then why try? To cap it, Jack Straw, barrister when not British Foreign Secretary, opines brazenly that it does not matter whether weapons are found. If you have no answer, guillotine the argument and retire hurt!

The White House is currently engaged in getting another resolution through the Security Council to lift

The Rest of the World!

sanctions. It was foreseen in earlier Caveats. The argument is simple. Sanctions limit the oil extracted and Cheney and gang are in a tearing hurry. It is now known that not only does Cheney's company, Halliburton have a contract to put out oil fires but having put them out, they will go on to extract and distribute the oil. It does not take a master of the art of argument to conclude that the more oil the company can pump the better Cheney and Bush will be pleased.

Here is an extract from the latest Bush Thesaurus of Words and Phrases.

1. **Terrorism:** Violent actions that hurt American interests real or imagined.

2. **Iraqi oil is for the Iraqi people:** After Bush, Cheney and Rumsfeld have had a go and the US has recouped itself for the cost of their private aggression launched against International Law, against expressed wishes of the United Nations and against all canons of civilized behaviour.

3. **Operation Iraqi Freedom:** Freedom for America, Britain and the 'Coalition of the Willing', including paragons like Azerbaijan, Eritrea, Ethiopia, Georgia and Uzbekistan to inflict horrendous damage, massive civilian casualties and widespread loot. According to Rumsfeld, these are mere manifestations of the new freedoms gifted by America!

4. **Iraqi face for the interim administration:** Will be installed as soon as America can find a quisling with an Iraqi face and an American brain.

5. **Weapons of Mass Destruction:** Easier to say what they are not. They are not the nuclear bombs dropped on Hiroshima and Nagasaki in 1945. Not the Tomahawk cruise missiles launched from safe distances. Not the cluster bombs designed to cause maximum civilian casualties. Not 2,000 lb bombs, which cause huge craters and obliterate anything to do with Saddam Hussein. Bush now says Saddam may have 'destroyed', hidden or exported the weapons. If he destroyed them, he is still 'in material breach', as he needed American permission to do what the Security Council wanted him to do anyway.

6. **A pivotal role for the UN:** Any role delegated by the United States, i.e. collect cash for the war, allow pillage of Iraqi oil by lifting sanctions, distribute humanitarian aid paid for by sales of Iraqi oil after priorities listed in (2), above are met.

7. **Catastrophic Success:** All of the foregoing for which the Iraqi people are declared to be duly grateful as recorded in the Oval Office of the White House with a copy for ready reference in the Pentagon.

Bush said from the aircraft carrier *Abraham Lincoln* — "God, continue to Bless America!" When will He Bless the rest of the world instead!

16 May 2003

Epilogue

The question is on everybody's lips. Will America and Britain come to their senses and in this hopeful scenario, how long will it take? To probe alternatives and reach conclusions, however tentative, it is necessary to understand the kind of mind that President Bush brings to bear upon his office. It is a closed mind, a dreadful affliction. He believes with a religious faith that he can do no wrong and never makes a mistake. The religious right in America to which President Bush belongs is as dangerous as Osama bin Laden's belief in his version of fundamentalism. Osama's fanaticism is religious bigotry and the power that can go with it. Bush is no less a fanatic but his fanaticism is tempered with a concern for political power for its own sake coupled with a conviction that he is God's gift to the American people. Osama uses the vast wealth at his disposal to do God's work on earth, as he understands it. Bush holds that wealth is for himself, his friends and his cronies who have bankrolled his election and he must repay; never mind if in the process he goes after oil that does not belong to him or his country. To that extent he is in the grip of his handlers, Rumsfeld, Cheney and Perle—the last had to resign his powerful position in the Pentagon on a conflict of interest charge but manages to continue as Rumsfeld's consultant.

There is also the underlining urge to avenge September 11 on anyone, anywhere and in any manner and to wipe out the humiliation suffered in Viet Nam. The United States will not be denied. Hysteria and jingoism have submerged liberal values and rules of civilised intercourse and brought out the worst in the collective psyche of the American people. Bush has gone to ridiculous lengths to justify the wholly illegal and outrageous attack on Iraq. First it was WMD or weapons of mass destruction, which were presumed to exist against all the evidence. They simply had to be found. In the process, discloses Hans Blix, the chief weapons inspector, in an interview on BBC television on 22 April 2003, 'forged documents were pressed into service, and in a variety of ways US officials set out to discredit the UN's weapons inspectors to win Council support for military action'. This is a damning indictment. Iraq's 12,000 page report required by the weapons inspectors is literally hijacked by the United States, which blandly announces that it will look at it first and give copies to everybody else in the Security Council afterwards. Without even a cursory examination, it is damned as old, incomplete, a rehash, and useless. National Security Adviser, Condoleezza Rice another member of the loony right around Bush is directed to see Hans Blix ahead of the next report he is making to the Security Council, to ensure that he holds Saddam in material breach of his obligations. Confident that she could not be denied, a news item is fabricated and put out detailing what Blix would say the next day. Blix

Epilogue

ignores the crude pressure but the effort *was* made. Now Bush is hoist with his own petard. Russia says sanctions cannot be lifted, simply because Bush desires to make a meal of Iraqi oil, until the weapons inspectors either find the weapons or certify that they do not exist. Never the one to admit he has been outfoxed, Bush intones that he is satisfied that Saddam would have got himself a weapons system within six months if he had not been overthrown! We have a glimpse here of what comes naturally to a closed mind.

Tony Blair, being an accessory before, during and after the fact, is a bigger disappointment because much better was expected of him. As a politician he had turned his Labour Party round into a winning and credible organisation. He is a barrister by training and should be familiar with the art of argument. Yet he fabricates material left by somebody on a web site to make out a case for Saddam holding weapons of mass destruction. His introduction to the official British publication, released with appropriate fanfare, insists it is based on secret intelligence reports, prompting the question—if it was secret what was it doing on the Internet anyway! British cabinet ministers have regularly tried to intimidate the BBC for what is said to be interference with the public's perception of the war.

If this is the background, what is the prognosis? In both Britain and America the economy is likely to force a return to sanity ahead of argument or a sense of guilt. Bush wants sanctions to be lifted so that oil can flow freely to American companies like Bechtel and Dick Cheney's company wanting to put out oil well fires. The debate in the Security Council is going to be interesting. France is being bludgeoned into supporting the lifting of sanctions after a fashion, but there is Russia and a majority of the Council to consider. It takes $2 billion a month to keep the pampered American GI in Iraq. Out of the Budget of $74.5 billion voted by the US Congress only $2.4 billion is for reconstruction. Over $1 billion is already committed to Bechtel and Cheney's Oil Well Fires firm. These contracts are awarded by the USAID. To the extent that this is an American agency, it raises no cavil. But the real question is—where will the replenishment come from? America is hoping that having caused the horrendous death and destruction—all without just cause—the rest of the world will rush in to clean up after them. It is a vain hope.

There are other straws in the wind. Politically, American intelligence has been grossly over-optimistic. They expected the majority Shias to come out with cups of tea in welcome because they were told that Saddam being a Sunni was not a favourite of theirs. As America's General Garner was holding his meeting with Iraqi quislings, 20,000 Shias assembled spontaneously and demanded that America get out of Iraq—Shias and Sunnis would settle their differences later. Iraq is not Afghanistan. Then there is always Saddam. Technology could overhear his whispered conversation with his sons and friends from way up high and four 2,000, pound bombs were rained on the spot but Saddam is alive. Even Bush admits this as he warns Saddam 'not to pop his head up'. Ordinary Americans must be ashamed of the language used by their President, even though he did not win a popular mandate to represent them.

In the coming weeks and months America will tire of keeping its forces in Iraq especially as they are not welcome and it costs too much. They are trying to install a quisling of doubtful reputation, Ahmad Chalabi who is himself not sure whether he can survive. This is bound to lead in the fairly short term to some sort of a UN mandate to run the country. The UN must then call its price. An

Epilogue

interim administration, law and order, a police force, reconstruction and repair of the dreadful damage caused must all be under a clear and firm UN presence. The objective must be to get American troops out of Iraq as soon as possible and sooner than that! To be fair to both America and Britain public opposition to the war as being illegal and unnecessary has been strong in most large cities. It will grow in geometrical progression when the boys come home. There is a feeling that criticism 'while our boys are out there is not done'.

Here is a check-list of objectives that the UN must work on to restore Iraq's sovereignty:

1. Prevent America from getting its dirty paws on Iraqi oil. If necessary use the Russian veto to stop them from bullying the Security Council into lifting sanctions until weapons inspectors return and report that they have found the weapons or that there are, and have been none.
2. Get American and British troops out of Iraq. They are not welcome and they are frightened of suicide bombers and resultant casualties even after the fighting has ended, so it should be easier than we think.
3. The UN mandate must include complete control of all aspects of governance in Iraq; there will be resistance here. Powell has already limited the UN to humanitarian assistance adding that America has spent billions on this war. This clearly betrays a desire, nay determination, to reimburse themselves from the proceeds of Iraqi oil and then march forward to enrich themselves and their accomplices.

4. Stabilising Iraq after the horrendous damage and loss of life will be a challenge worthy of the UN. Quislings will not do. Iraq is a secular state although Bush is responsible for Saddam Hussein calling for a *jihad* out of desperation.
5. If there is any justice in this world America and Britain should be made to pay for the entire cost of reconstruction. In an imperfect world this may not be possible. However it is entirely possible to ensure that reconstruction contracts are open to international bidding under UN auspices, unless the USA in a sudden attack of conscience, makes itself responsible without looking for reimbursement from Iraqi oil proceeds.
6. President Clinton has intervened in a most effective manner. I have dealt with this in the Caveat—*In the sands of Time!* of 20 April 2003. He is a consummate politician and has a first class mind. He will act as a catalyst to remind America of what it has been and can be again. He is waiting for American troops to come home. Bush can't keep them there indefinitely.

And so all things considered I remain optimistic. If Saddam is alive, he will surface at a time of his choosing. But it is too speculative to consider the possibility. Let it rest. I am more concerned about making sure that the world's only superpower can come into its own again. Two curators of American museums have resigned in protest at the failure to protect Iraq's priceless treasures of antiquity. It was the American Chapter of Amnesty International that blew the whistle on the deliberate targeting of foreign journalists in Baghdad and they did not mince words. Tony Blair is unlikely to recover from the blow to his credulity and his competence. He can be left to the judgment of the mature British nation. I will be content if nemesis ensures that George W Bush, who never lost sight of his re-election campaign even as he indulged in the grossest of gross abuses of International Law and gave free reign of his spurious religious convictions, does not carry a single State of the Union, in trying to benefit from the miseries he has inflicted so wantonly, on hapless civilians with his weapons of mass destruction. Who knows? If the trial of Slobodan Milosevic can be completed soon, Justices at the International Court of Justice in The Hague will not be without work!

Thus should break the dawn!

IRAQ – OVER THE YEARS

Modern Iraq has had a troubled history. Following is a snapshot of the main events:

25 April 1920	Iraq is placed under British mandate after the collapse of the Ottoman Empire.
October 1920	A provisional Arab Council of State, advised by British officials, is established, replacing military rule.
23 August 1921	Faisal ibn Hussain, former Hashemite king of Syria, is crowned king.
3 October 1932	Iraq becomes independent and joins the League of Nations. Britain retains use of two air bases.
February 1963	Baath Party seizes power in military coup and Kassem is killed. Abd Salam Mohammed Aref is installed as President.
November 1963	President Aref ousts Baathists.
March 1974	Iraq announces implementation of 1970 autonomy agreement with the Kurds. Dissatisfied Kurds renew fighting.
16 July 1979	Saddam Hussein takes power.

16 March 1988	Iraq attacks northern Kurdish town of Halabja which had been seized by Iran. About 5,000 people were killed.
20 August 1988	UN ceasefire effectively ends Iran-Iraq war.
2 August 1990	Iraq invades Kuwait.
6 August 1990	Security Council imposes sanctions on Iraq-occupied Kuwait.
April–May 1990	US, British and French troops create safe haven in north to protect returning refugees. Iraqi troops withdraw. Allied troops patrol 'no-fly' zone in north.
11 April 1990	UN declares Gulf War ceasefire.
June 1990	UN arms inspectors begin work. Disputes over Iraq's compliance with UN demands for the scrapping of its chemical, biological, nuclear and ballistic arms programmes leads to successive crises and keeps sanctions in place.
May 1996	Iraq accepts 'Oil for Food' deal with UN.
30 January 2002	US President brands Iraq, along with Iran and North Korea, part of an 'axis of evil'.
12 September 2002	Bush urges UN to force Iraq to disarm. UN inspectors resume work after 4-year break.

15 March 2003	Saddam puts Iraq on a war footing, dividing the country into four military districts and putting his younger son Qusay in command of Baghdad-Tikrit area.
17 March 2003	USA, Britain and Spain abandon efforts to get international endorsement for war against Saddam Hussein. Bush gives Saddam 48 hours to leave country.
18 March 2003	Iraq rejects Bush's ultimatum.
20 March 2003	USA starts war to oust Saddam Hussein.

BREAKING NEWS

20 March 2003: USA attacks Iraq

After a failed missile strike aimed at eliminating Iraqi President Saddam Hussein early today to open hostilities, America began a massive bombardment of Baghdad and launched a ground offensive late tonight.

THE WORLD REACTS

MIDDLE EAST & ISRAEL: Arab nations demand the withdrawal of US and British troops from Iraq. Israel's security establishment on maximum alert.

FRANCE: French President Jacques Chirac says France "regrets this action taken without UN approval and hopes that it won't cause "humanitarian catastrophe".

GERMANY: German Foreign Minister expresses its dismay over the war.

RUSSIA: Russian President Vladimir Putin calls on the USA to stop the war, terming the campaign "a serious political mistake".

CHINA: China demands that military action against Iraq be stopped immediately and said that the initial attack was "violating the norms of international behaviour".

USA: Police arrested 1,000 people in San Francisco as tens of thousands protested across America against US war against Iraq.

BREAKING NEWS	THE WORLD REACTS
23 March 2003: Basra airport & bridge captured, Umm Qasr and Nasiriyan fall Allied forces have captured oilfields and other key sites in the south-eastern areas of Basra and Nasiriyan and have taken almost complete control of southern Iraq, including the key port of Umm Qasr, as well as Basra, Iraq's second-largest city.	*MIDDLE EAST & ISRAEL:* Thousands of Arabs seething with anger about a heavy US-led bombing of Baghdad protest amid concerns that the demonstrations could threaten stability in the volatile region. *RUSSIA:* Foreign minister Igor Ivanov accuses USA of stepping on Russia's economic interests in Iraq.
25 March 2003: US breaches bridge to Baghdad US Marines finally punched past Iraqi resistance to cross Euphrates river at Nasiriyan.	*MIDDLE EAST & ISRAEL:* Pockets of Iraqi resistance generate a lot of Arab pride. In Saudi Arabia, unlike Egypt or Jordan, there is no public manifestation of resentment, yet feeling is as strong as anywhere else. *FRANCE:* Demonstrators in Paris smash windows of McDonald restaurant. *GERMANY:* German restaurants say 'nein' to all things American. No more Coca-Cola or Budweiser, no Marlboro, no American whisky or even American Express cards—a growing number of restaurants are taking

BREAKING NEWS	THE WORLD REACTS
	everything American off their menus to protest against the war in Iraq.
USA: Police arrest two Nobel Peace Prize winners, Mairead Corrigan Maguire, who won the prize in 1976 for peace activism in North Ireland conflict and Jody Williams, a 1997 winner for her work to ban landmines, along with more than 30 other people protesting near the White House.
31 March 2003: US bombers blitz Baghdad

Even as Iraq promised to turn the desert into a graveyard for coalition forces, US central command retaliates with a blitzkrieg involving three generations of US long-range bombers—the Cold War workhorse B-52, the controversial B-1 and the delta-winged stealth B-2. | *MIDDLE EAST & ISRAEL:* Syria reiterates its support for Iraq and its people against what it says are an 'illegitimate' US invasion. Iran rejects US accusations that it has deployed militants into neighbouring Iraq. Iran's foreign minister, Kamal Kharrazi said that Tehran would oppose any government imposed by US on Baghdad.
UK: Public support for the war against Iraq has fallen for the first time in Britain since the conflict began. According to polls 54% believed it was right to take military action. |

BREAKING NEWS	THE WORLD REACTS
5 April 2003: **Allied troops take Saddam airport** US troops take Saddam International airport renaming it Baghdad International airport.	*FRANCE:* "What is surprising is that the airport was not destroyed by the Iraqis. ... It's the same with bridges." (Francis Gere, French defence analyst) *GERMANY:* Germany and Russia call for rapid end to hostilities and agree on the leading role of the UN in administering Iraq after the war. *RUSSIA:* "The battle for Baghdad will last approximately one month unless there is a secret agreement to surrender. The airport has strategic importance to Americans as they will be able to fly military hardware." (Sergei Sumbayev, commentator for *Krasnaya Zvezda*, Russian army newspaper, Moscow) *USA:* Michel Kelly, editor at large for *The Atlantic Monthly* and columnist for The *Washington Post,* killed in Iraq. He is the first US journalist to die in the war.
7 April 2003: Baghdad battle reaches streets American forces storm	*MIDDLE EAST & ISRAEL:* Arabs react with dismay and disbelief to television images of US tanks in the heart of Baghdad, with

BREAKING NEWS	THE WORLD REACTS
Saddam Hussein's main presidential palace in the heart of Baghdad amid bloody firefights.	some dismissing the news as American propaganda and others signing up for *jihad*.

8 April 2003: Coalition strikes kill 3 journalists

An American tank fired at Palestine Hotel, where several hundred journalists are staying, killing two cameramen and wounding three others. Less than a kilometre away, another journalist died when an *Al-Jazeera TV* office was hit from the air in a US bombing run.

MIDDLE EAST & ISRAEL: Jordan receives its first Iraqi refugees after nearly three weeks of war—a mother and son.

FRANCE: French President Jacques Chirac says that it is up to the UN alone to take on the political, humanitarian and economic reconstruction of Iraq.

RUSSIA: Following the Bush-Blair 'war council' in Belfast, Russian President Vladimir Putin summons 'counter-war council' in St Petersburg this weekend to intensify diplomatic efforts for post-war dispension. French President Jacques Chirac, German leader Gerhard Schroedar and UN Secretary General Kofi Annan are likely to attend.

9 April 2003: America & anarchy march in

Saddam Hussein's rule over Iraq crumbled today as American forces swept

MIDDLE EAST & ISRAEL: Arabs watched in disbelief as Saddam Hussein, described by one Moroccan as the 'best dictator', lost Baghdad to US-led forces without a fight.

BREAKING NEWS	THE WORLD REACTS
into the heart of chaotic Baghdad, toppling a huge statue of the man portrayed by many western governments as evil incarnate. He towered over the country for 24 years. But Saddam Hussein remains elusive to the last.	*GERMANY:* A group of German university professors, angered by the US-British war against Iraq, have launched a campaign to replace many popular English-language words used in Germany with French terms.
	UK: A badly burnt Iraqi boy, who lost his family and both arms in a US bombing raid on Baghdad has become the face of the suffering in the war. This has sparked a flood of fund-raising appeals.
12 April 2003: Saddam Hussein's top scientific advisor surrenders General Amer Hammoudi al-Saadi, one of the 55 people on America's most wanted leaders of Iraq surrenders to US forces in Baghdad.	*MIDDLE EAST & ISRAEL:* Pentagon advisor Richard Perle, a key architect of the US-led drive to oust Saddam Hussein, says that Syria will be a possible military target if it is found harbouring Iraqi weapons of mass destruction and sheltering Saddam Hussein or his relatives.

BREAKING NEWS	THE WORLD REACTS
13 April 2003: Coalition storms Saddam's last bastion US Marines today entered Tikrit, Saddam's hometown and last bastion.	*MIDDLE EAST & ISRAEL:* Israeli Prime Minister Ariel Sharon says the US-led war on Iraq "generated a shock through the Middle East and it brings with it a prospect of great changes. … . The Arab world, in general, and the Palestinians in particular, have been shaken." *RUSSIA:* "The capture of Baghdad may go down in history as one of the fastest and most successful military operations in urban conditions. The predictions of most analysts that Iraqis could create a 'second Stalingrad' were wrong." (*Vremya* Novostei, Moscow) *UK:* "Anyone who thinks this war is over is not living in a real world. The task ahead is huge. Far greater than overcoming a ragged army and deposing a hated ruler. … Now Saddam has gone, we want to see this tragic country helped into a peaceful, fear-free life. But we also want our troops back home as quickly as possible." (*The Daily Mirror*, London)

BREAKING NEWS	THE WORLD REACTS
15 April 2003: Iraq weighs guided democracy Iraqi political and religious leaders hold talks on their country's future with US and British officials and pledged to work for a democratic, federal Iraq.	*MIDDLE EAST & ISRAEL:* Arabs are unnerved and insulted by US accusations that Syria is a 'rogue nation' developing chemical weapons and fear Washington's stream of broadsides mean the war on Iraq could extend to other Arab States. However, Arab leaders of countries like Jordan, the smaller Gulf States, Egypt which discreetly or publicly felicitated the US-led campaign against Iraq can expect political and financial rewards. *FRANCE, GERMANY & RUSSIA:* The 'Non-Nyet-Nein' coalition of France, Russia and Germany are staking their individual claims to a role in shaping and profiting from the new Iraq, moving to build bridges to the USA and Britain. France says it wants to be pragmatic; Germany says it is an honest broker because it has no economic interests in Iraq; Russia says it will consider Washington's call to forgive some $8 billion in Soviet era debt.

BREAKING NEWS

18 April 2003:
Iraqis cry for Islamic State, asks US to go

Muslims poured out of mosques and into the streets of Baghdad, calling for an Islamic State to be established.

25 April 2003:
Bush backtracks on Iraq weapons

After an unsuccessful search of several sites where the CIA was confident the USA would find WMD, President Bush has hinted that these weapons may never be found.

27 April 2003:
Rumour flies thick & fast after surrender of Deputy Prime Minister Tariq Aziz

The former Iraqi Deputy Prime Minister Tariq Aziz ranks 43rd on the US list of 55 most wanted Iraqis. US interrogates him, hoping to get information on Saddam and his two sons.

THE WORLD REACTS

MIDDLE EAST & ISRAEL: Stunned by the swift US-led takeover of Iraq, neighbouring States gather in Saudi Arabia to weigh a response and discuss ties with future authorities in Baghdad.